Patterns for a
New Testament Church

Patterns for a
New Testament Church

CECIL RAY TAYLOR

WIPF & STOCK · Eugene, Oregon

PATTERNS FOR A NEW TESTAMENT CHURCH

Wipf & Stock
An Imprint of Wipf and Stock Publishers
199 W. 8th Ave., Suite 3
Eugene, OR 97401

www.wipfandstock.com

PAPERBACK ISBN: 979-8-3852-5118-6
HARDCOVER ISBN: 979-8-3852-5119-3
EBOOK ISBN: 979-8-3852-5120-9

06/10/25

Dedicated to
the great love of my life,
my precious wife Reeda Acuff Taylor,
my "travel buddy" who co-led dozens
of short-term student mission trips
and nine tours of Israel,
and who constantly challenges me
in following Christ the King!

Contents

Introduction

WHAT IS A NEW Testament church? To this question, two common answers are given. The Roman Catholic Church claims it is the New Testament church because it can trace an unbroken line of descent all the way back to the first century. Although it now may look very little like that church, Roman Catholics claim to be the New Testament church because of historical *continuity*.

On the other hand, Protestants claim that what makes a church a New Testament church is *conformity* to the teachings and practices of the New Testament. If every church in the world went out of business today, a group of believers could start a New Testament church tomorrow by adopting the faith and practices of the first-century churches as the New Testament sets them forth.

If the Protestant answer is right, as I believe, it is imperative to know what first-century churches believed and how they behaved. What they believed is a topic for another time. The focus here falls on how New Testament churches behaved because their character and actions set patterns for building future New Testament churches.

Somewhere in the edge of the Brazilian rainforest near Porto Velho, Rondonia, two thousand miles up the Amazon right at the foothills of the Bolivian mountains, stands a Baptist chapel. In it are pews and a pulpit I built in 1995. I cut the boards. I screwed the pieces together. I varnished the furniture. Understand that I spent my life as a preacher and a professor, not a carpenter. I had never done anything like that job before. But our construction team leader gave me the job. He did not write out instructions. He handed me some patterns and a power saw. I just followed the patterns and produced the pews and pulpit.

The present work tries to find patterns for building a New Testament church in the descriptions of selected churches mentioned in the New Testament. It does not include the letters to the seven churches of the book of Revelation because scores of books have been written about those congregations.

Some may question why there is no mention of the issue of single or plural elders.[1] The answer is that the New Testament evidence is ambiguous. For sure, some churches (e.g., Jerusalem in Acts 15:2, 4, 22–23; and possibly Ephesus in Acts 20:17) had more than one elder. But the New Testament does not indicate that every congregation had multiple elders. The closest it comes are Luke's report that Paul and Barnabas appointed "elders in every church" ("according to a church," *kata ekklesian*; Acts 14:23) and Paul's directive to Titus to appoint "elders in every town" (*kata polin*, Titus 1:5). Commentators commonly say Acts 14:23 means Paul and his colleague Barnabas appointed more than one elder in each and every church in that area of southern Asia Minor. But the language may rather indicate that, moving "from church to church," they appointed at least one elder in each. Also, Paul's instruction for Titus to appoint "elders in every town" (*kata polin*) in Crete (Titus 1:5) may also mean that Titus was to appoint at least one elder

1. In the New Testament, the terms "elder" (*presbuteros*), "overseer" (*episkopos*) or "bishop," and "shepherd" (*poimen*) are synonyms applied to a specific group of church officers. In Acts 20:17–35, Luke referred to the leaders of the church at Ephesus as "elders" (Acts 20:17) and Paul labeled them as "overseers" (Acts 20:28). The verb (*poimainein*) that follows "overseers," the English Standard Version (ESV) translates as "to care for the church of God," that is, to do the work of a shepherd in tending his flock. Perhaps it is better rendered "be shepherds" or "pastors." That "shepherd" is another way to say "pastor," the ESV acknowledges in a note attached to Eph 4:11. The same usage occurs in 1 Pet 5:1–2 where that apostle applied "elder" and "bishop" to a fixed set of church leaders and urged them to "shepherd" the flock God entrusted to them. In this reference, "shepherd" (*poimanate*) is just a different form of the same Greek verb in Acts 20:28.

in each city on the island. To illustrate this point, a news story might report that "John Kingman distributed political yard signs in his neighborhood from house to house." Clearly this sentence is ambiguous. It might mean John left multiple signs in the yard at each house, but it could just as well mean that he left one sign in the yard of each house. Either sense satisfies the syntax. The statements in Acts and Titus are ambiguous in exactly the same way. The language fits a plurality of churches each served by a single elder, as well as it fits a plurality of elders serving a single church. Because the issue remains indefinite, it is not considered part of any pattern.

The following list of patterns is exemplary, not exhaustive. Many more could be identified. Not everyone will agree with the author's reading of the biblical evidence, but surely everyone can profit from engaging with the ideas presented here.

Now, on to the search for patterns!

Chapter 1

The Master's Church
A Word from the Founder

IN THE SHADOW OF Mount Hermon near Caesarea Philippi Jesus asked his disciples, "Who do men say that I am?" (Matt 16:13). That question was not hard to answer. People everywhere were talking about Jesus. In fact, they were saying genuinely great things about him. Some declared he was the late John the Baptist, lately beheaded by Herod Antipas but now risen from the dead. Others insisted he was Elijah, the greatest of Israel's prophets. Most Jews expected him to return to herald the day of the Lord (Mal 4:5). Still others claimed he was Jeremiah. The rabbis said Jeremiah hid the ark of the covenant and the altar of incense in secret caves when Babylon destroyed Jerusalem in 586 BC (2 Macc 1:1–12). They looked for him to return in the last days to restore those treasures and bring God's glory again to Israel. Or, if they hesitated to say Jesus was as great as John, Elijah, or Jeremiah, at the least the people thought him "one of the prophets," a man on whom the spirit of prophecy rested, a servant to whom God revealed his secrets (Amos 3:7).

But Jesus pressed on to life's most important question. Of the disciples he demanded, "But who do you say that I am?" Peter

1

answered, "You are the Christ, the Messiah of Israel, the Son of the living God!" To this point, no one had said this about Jesus, but Peter did. And Jesus replied, "You are right. But no man told you this truth and you did not figure it out on your own. God showed you this!" (Matt 16:15–17).

Then, for the first time, Jesus revealed that he intended to build a church. Some think the church is not important, but it is. Jesus founded it! In the Old Testament (LXX) the nation of Israel was God's *ekklesia* ("assembly"), a group of people he chose for himself (Deut 18:16; 23:2; Ps 22:25). Here, Jesus stated his plan to "build" his own community of followers (Matt 16:13–20). Jesus laid out a trio of important facts about his church using three symbols: rock, keys, and gates.

ITS FOUNDATION: THE ROCK

"On this rock I will build my church" (Matt 16:18). Many say Simon Peter is the rock the church rests on, but they badly misunderstand Jesus. First, had Jesus meant Peter was the foundation of the church it would be far more natural for him to say, "You are Peter and upon you I will build my church." Jesus could have said this, but he did not. Second, historically it was James, not Peter, who led the first-century church. Third, in his first letter, Peter called Jesus the foundation of the church, "the cornerstone" (1 Pet 2:4–7). The man to whom Jesus spoke these words said the rock was Jesus! Finally, Matthew was there that day and heard Jesus speak. When he wrote this account, the apostle chose his words carefully to make it clear that Jesus did not mean he would build his church on Peter. The Aramaic Jesus spoke had only one word for stone (*kephas*), but Matthew used two Greek words to show Jesus did not say Peter was the foundation of the church. In Greek, "Peter" (masculine gender, *petros*) means "a stone." But for "this rock," Matthew used a different word—*petra* (feminine gender), "a ledge of rock." It is too bad that printed text does not preserve voice inflections or gestures. I cannot prove it, but Jesus may well have gestured to himself or with some other motion indicating his meaning. "Peter, you are a small rock and, along with all who confess me as Christ and Son of God, you will be part of the church I will build. But it is on this massive ledge of rock, on myself, that I will build my church!" Matthew took pains to make this clear when he wrote down the episode in his Gospel! The church's lone foundation is Jesus Christ! After he quit the carpenter shop in Nazareth, the Lord built only one thing. That was his church!

When engineers began drawing plans for the 1,250-foot-tall Empire State Building in the 1930s, skeptics scoffed. "It cannot be done. You cannot stack 102 stories of steel and concrete on top of each other and expect the building to stand." But the engineers were confident. "If we can make the foundation deep enough and strong enough, there is no limit to the height we can raise this building."[1] They dug the foundation deep. They made it strong. They put up the building. And still it stands!

Twenty centuries have proved Jesus Christ is a foundation deep enough and strong enough to support his church. This much is sure. No other foundation will do. Some congregations build their church on a special pastor. But when that pastor dies, moves on, or messes up, a church founded on him falters, fractures, or fails. Others build their church on a special program, e.g., music, drama, youth, recreation, or television. But when the program goes flat, the church declines. I know a church that built on a certain wealthy deacon, sure that if he left the church it would fail. They chose the wrong foundation!

The foundation of a New Testament church is Jesus Christ. All else is sinking sand! Does your church rest on him or on someone or something else?

ITS FUNCTION: THE KEYS

Alex Haley wrote *Roots: The Saga of an American Family*, the epic story of his family descended from an African slave, Kunta Kinte. I heard a story once about Alex's father, Simon. According to the

1. Powell, *Church Today*, 18.

story, Simon earned his bachelor's degree from Lane College in Jackson, Tennessee, and then went away to Cornell University for a master's degree in agriculture. In the process, Simon earned a Phi Beta Kappa key in recognition of his academic achievements. Back in Tennessee for a family gathering in Henning, just west of Jackson, admiring relatives gathered around while Simon talked to them about the process of his education. Simon called attention to the tiny key he wore on a chain on his vest, explained that it was given to only a select few, and told how hard he had worked to get it. Later that day, an aunt eased over next to her young nephew. "Son, can I ask you a question about that little key? What does it open?"

Keys open doors. Jesus gave Peter some keys (Matt 16:19). He left no doubt what these keys opened. They were the keys that open the door to the kingdom of God so people can go in (e.g., Luke 11:52). Later in this very Gospel, Jesus rebuked the scribes and Pharisees because they not only refused to enter the kingdom of God for themselves but they also took away the keys of knowledge to keep others from entering (Matt 23:13). The keys of the kingdom gave access for others to enter God's kingdom through the very doors by which Peter himself had entered. By preaching the gospel, Peter (and other disciples) used these keys to "open a door of faith" (Acts 14:27), not only to the Jews (Acts 2) but also to the Samaritans (Acts 8) and to the gentiles (Acts 20). The "keys of the kingdom" stand for the gospel-sharing, soul-winning function of the church, across the street and around the world.

Now the language about binding and loosing comes clear. The key verbs are future perfect passive in tense. Both require helping verbs in English. Not one in a hundred translations gets it right. The most comprehensive translation reads, "Whatever you forbid on earth must be already forbidden in heaven, and whatever you permit on earth must be already permitted in heaven."[2] It is not that heaven must do what the church on earth decides, but that the church can announce on earth only what heaven has already done! When a man enters the kingdom of God by faith in Jesus,

2. Williams, *New Testament*, note j at Matt 16:19.

God forgives his sin and the church can say to him, "Your sin is gone!" If a man refuses to enter, God refuses to forgive his sin and the church can say to him, "Your sin remains!" The church has no message of its own. It can only echo heaven's voice!

A New Testament church must *carry the keys* to the kingdom. No other keys can open the door to salvation and heaven. A New Testament church must *protect* these keys. A key has a unique shape. Its usefulness depends entirely on it keeping that shape. The church must "contend for the faith" (Jude 3) and let no one change its shape! But more, a New Testament church must *use* these keys! What is your church doing with the keys to the kingdom? Where are the members who have used them even once? Do they rust in people's pockets and purses? A New Testament church must get hold of the keys to the kingdom, contend for them, and put them to use!

ITS FUTURE: THE GATES

"The gates of hell shall not prevail against it" (Matt 16:18). In the original language of the New Testament the word for "hell" is *hades*. Unfortunately many versions render *hades* as "hell" here and throughout the New Testament. However, hades is not the hell of fire (*gehenna*). It is simply the "unseen" world, where people go when they die, whether saved or lost.

It was fitting that Jesus spoke of the "gates of hades" at Caesarea Philippi. He did not just pull this language out of thin air. At this ancient pagan site, visitors can see a cave that the Greeks and Romans said was the entrance to the underworld, the "gates of hades," the door to the realm of the dead. In Jesus' day the "gates of hades" meant the doors of death (Isa 38:10). The Lord said those doors will never close on his church. No matter how fierce the attacks on it, Christ's church will never die. Death can never bring it down.

One by one, the apostles were hunted down and killed, but the gates of hades did not prevail. Christ's church lived on. Early Christians were slain by droves, but Christ's church lived on!

In AD 303, Diocletian, emperor of Rome, launched a vicious attack on Christianity. He burned or buried hundreds of Scriptures and killed thousands of Christians in the empire's last, largest, and bloodiest official persecution. It is said that he ordered a column of triumph raised with the Latin inscription *Extincto nomine Christianorum*: "I have wiped out the name of Christians!" But it was Diocletian and the Roman Empire that died. Christ's church lived on.

Fast-forward to the early 1900s. China was the center of Christian missions. In 1949, Mao Tse-Tung seized power, expelled all Christian missionaries, and cracked down on Christianity. Radical communists buried hymnals and Bibles and burned houses of worship. They shot pastors or imprisoned and tortured them. Believers were ridiculed publicly and forced into labor camps or exiled to remote places. But when the door to China opened in recent years and the Western world got a peek inside, the view was startling! Not only had the church survived the all-out efforts to destroy it, it actually flourished. The number of believers in China swelled from four million in 1949 to something approaching fifty million today. Chairman Mao died. But Christ's church lives on!

In fact, the last enemy to be destroyed is death (1 Cor 15:26). Can I tell you something? On the day death dies, Christ's church will be there to conduct the funeral! Glory to God!

Certain religious groups claim the true church died out along the way and disappeared. They say God sent Joseph Smith or Alexander Campbell or some other leader to "restore" it. Think about it! If those folks are right, Jesus was wrong. If he was right, they are wrong. I will side with Jesus every time!

Local congregations may come and go, but the church of the Lord Jesus Christ lives on forever. Members of a local group of believers can make theirs a New Testament church by confidently giving time, talents, and treasure to the Lord through their church with confidence they are investing in something eternal. A New Testament church faces the future and moves forward with sure and steady steps, knowing it cannot fail!

There she stands! The church of Christ! A New Testament church is known by its foundation, its function, and its future!

No one just joins Christ's church. It is not a random collection of believers. Jesus builds his church, one by one! "The Lord added to their number day by day those who were being saved" (Acts 2:47). Still he does! Has he added you? Will you let him?

Are you using the keys of the kingdom? Or do they rust in your pockets? Do you face the future with the confidence that, come what may, you are investing your money, your family, indeed, your very life in something that is immortal? A New Testament church is one built by Jesus, using the keys to the kingdom and facing the future with confidence that it will live forever!

Chapter 2

The Mother Church
Jerusalem

THE JERUSALEM CONGREGATION WAS the first church and, for nearly ten years, the only one. It was in Jerusalem that the 120 disciples waited for the Father to keep his promise and send the Holy Spirit. In Jerusalem, they preached "the mighty works of God" (Acts 2:11) in recognizable languages (Acts 2:6, 8; *dialektos*, "dialects"), not in some supposed tongues unknown on earth. And the Lord added three thousand to his church (Acts 2:42). In Jerusalem, the Lord kept on building his church. How natural that, when new churches formed, they would look to the mother church as a model for faith and practice. Every church would do well to measure itself by the mother church and mold itself to be like her!

The opening chapters of Acts (1:12–26; 6:1–6) offer strong impressions about what it takes to be a New Testament church like the mother church in Jerusalem.

ITS FELLOWSHIP

A remarkably diverse group of people formed the Jerusalem church. The 120 were all Jews, but they were of many types. Mary, widow of

a poor carpenter from Nazareth, sat together with Joanna and Su-
sannah, aristocrats from Herod's court (Luke 8:1–3). Distinguished
scholars like Joseph of Arimathea and Nicodemus worshiped with
rough Galilean fishermen like Peter and Andrew, James, and John.
Simon the Zealot rubbed shoulders peacefully with Matthew, tax
collector for the Roman occupiers. Rich landowners like Joseph
of Cyprus and penniless people came together in the Jerusalem
church. Such people did not mix socially in the first century, but in
the church they melded into Christian community.

The day of Pentecost brought even greater diversity. Three
thousand people from widely-scattered areas and nations came
into the church. Broad differences of language and culture sepa-
rated them. Despite their differences, however, they became one.
They cared for each other. Each shared what he had with others.
When a large number of new believers stayed after Pentecost to
learn more about their newfound faith but ran out of money, the
church pooled its resources to meet their needs (Acts 4:34–35).
This was not communism because it was both voluntary and tem-
porary. It was love-sharing.

When this flood of people came into the church they did not
divide into Jews and Greeks, slaves and free, educated and un-
educated. They did not limit membership to whites or blacks or
browns. They did not form cliques based on personal preferences.
They did not fight over whether to use Israeli music or Italian tunes.
It did not matter what anybody wore to church, whether robes or
rags. Their theme was "we are family!" And family they were.

A friend dropped in on a rock concert one night to find out
why they were so attractive to young people. A dude at the door
explained, "Man, when we come together, we not black or white,
rich or poor. We all just one." That is what the world is dying to
find. They go to rock concerts and bars looking for real acceptance
and community!

To be a New Testament church, a congregation must get beyond color and age, single and married, rich and poor, tall and
short, fat and thin! It must develop the spirit of oneness and practice authentic fellowship!

ITS POLITY

The Jerusalem church operated as a spiritual democracy under the lordship of Jesus. It had no boss but Christ and managed its own affairs under his direction. They had apostles, prophets, pastors, and deacons but authority rested in the hands of the congregation. Two examples make the point.

When Judas's suicide cut the twelve disciples to eleven, they did not appoint or even nominate a replacement. To the eleven, Peter quoted the prophecy of David, applied it to the issue, and stated the qualifications for the office (Acts 1:15–22). But he did not make the choice or even try to influence it. The record is clear. The apostles turned over the matter to the whole company of men and women. The church body found two who met the qualifications: Barsabas and Matthias. Then the congregation asked the Lord to show them which of those men he wanted to fill the vacancy. They wrote Matthias on one bit of broken pottery and Barsabas on another. These pieces they placed in an urn and shook it until Matthias' name fell out. Leave to one side the question of whether this was the right way to find the Lord's will. Clearly the 120 felt free to conduct business as a spiritual democracy. So Matthias "was numbered with" the eleven (Acts 1:26). That is a weak translation. In the original language the word *sugkatepsephisthe* may mean "harmoniously (or unanimously) voted in." Unanimity cannot be insisted on but the vote is clear. The Greek word means "to be chosen by a vote."[1] By a show of hands, the congregation installed Matthias as an apostle alongside the eleven.

Even when the Jerusalem church grew to thousands of members, they did business in the same congregational, democratic way. The apostles did not select or even nominate the first deacons. Instead, they threw the matter on the whole church. Acts 6:1–6 contains seven references showing that the whole congregation chose the men. "And the Twelve summoned the full number of the disciples. . . . Pick out from among you . . . and what they did pleased the whole gathering and they chose. . . . These they set

1. Rogers and Rogers, *Linguistic and Exegetical Key*, 231.

before the apostles, and they prayed and laid their hands on them." Plainly the church membership governed itself.

A New Testament church functions as a congregational democracy. Democracy is often inefficient and sometimes messy. But Churchill was spot on when he commented, "Democracy is the worst form of Government except for all those other forms."[2] And democracy is the New Testament way to do church. The more a pastor or elders control things, the less that church is a New Testament church. The more deacons run things, the less that church is a New Testament church. The more a church does away with business meetings and delegates all business to pastors, elders, committees, or official boards, the less that church is a New Testament church. The more members avoid business meetings, the less that church is a New Testament church. As a pastor, I used to apologize to visitors who showed up on a Wednesday night for our monthly business meeting. I stopped doing that. Instead, I started explaining that a business meeting is not just a necessary evil to keep the wheels rolling. It is the theological exercise of the priesthood of the believers. It is a matter of faith and practice. It is a New Testament way of doing things. To be a New Testament church, a congregation must act as a spiritual democracy under the lordship of Jesus!

ITS WORSHIP

The worship of the Jerusalem church was strikingly simple. Note first that it involved being "all together in one place" (Acts 2:1, 44). This is the natural flow of the spiritual life. Believers want to be with other believers for encouragement, comfort, and support.

In Istanbul, in March 2005, I listened to some missionaries boast about having three, fifteen-member house churches scattered in that city of millions. When I returned in July bringing a university missions team, I found all those believers meeting together in one place in a hotel near Taksim Square. The Turkish Christians had demanded to get together. And that Sunday there

---

2. International Churchill Society, "Worst Form of Government."

were not just forty-five of them but ninety! At times there may be good reasons to use multiple worship services and small house churches, but a church must resist, as long as possible, reversing the natural desire of Christians to be together.

Jerusalem Christians gathered for church wherever they could meet, e.g., in private homes, in borrowed synagogues, on temple porches and steps, on beaches, in vacant lots, and in gardens. What did their worship look like? That question finds an answer in Acts 2:42. Worship consisted of "the apostles' teaching." The apostles' doctrine now is preserved in the New Testament documents. A New Testament church makes much of the Bible in its worship. It makes room in its worship for reading Scripture. Its members devote themselves to study of the Bible in small groups. Recently, a Jehovah's Witness leader asked me if Baptists still taught the Bible in their churches. He said he and his group had begun to notice abysmal ignorance of the Bible among Baptist people who join them. What a stinging rebuke! A New Testament church makes much of the Bible in its worship.

Worship included "fellowship" (*koinonia*), which here means giving directed by the Holy Spirit (Acts 2:42). At times, this may involve giving money. Paul thanked the Philippians for their "partnership (*koinonia*) . . . in giving and receiving" (Phil 4:15). That is, they sent love gifts to support his missionary endeavors. One Wednesday night I visited the Peninsula Bible Church in Palo Alto, California, for what they called "a body life" service. Before they passed the offering plates, the pastor said, "If you have something to give, give. If you need something, take!" The plates came back empty. The body had met each of its members' needs!

However, sharing to meet others' needs may go beyond giving cash. In that same service at Peninsula Bible Church, a young college student stood up and said, "Tomorrow is Thanksgiving Day. I need to get to Los Angeles but there are no seats left on planes, trains, or buses." Across the auditorium a fellow member rose to say, "I have two cars. One of them is yours to use. See me after church to get the keys!" That is fellowship in its New Testament sense! A New Testament church makes much of sharing in its worship.

Worship included "the breaking of bread," i.e., a technical term for observing the Lord's Supper. A New Testament church makes much of joining Jesus at his table. The Supper should always be the focal point when it is observed, not just tacked on to the end of a "regular" service. Table fellowship played an important role in the early church. Eating is an intimate act. That is why men ask women to dinner on a date. Eating together builds intimacy with Jesus and with each other!

Worship involved "the prayers" (Acts 2:42). I loved it when, at our church in Mobile, Alabama, the choir sang the little chorus "Someone Is Praying for You," and people came to the altar to kneel in prayer for others there and elsewhere. The deacons led the way and the members followed. A New Testament church makes much of prayer in its worship.

In time, worship became complex and cluttered, but it was not always so. In the beginning it was simple, spontaneous, and sincere. In the mother church, they prayed, they sang psalms and hymns and spiritual songs, they read and preached the Scriptures, they gave invitations, and baptized converts.

First-century worship may not please twenty-first century believers. Some are leaving their simple churches looking for high church robes and drama, "bells and smells," and "sacred" dance. But there was none of that in the worship of the Jerusalem church. It was plain! It was simple! It was vanilla! It probably would not satisfy television junkies who would demand something more exciting and "professional." To entertain people these days, congregations call in a character who can play hymns on a handsaw or who can sing "God Bless America" while he stands on his head in the baptistry. I heard a story about a church that brought in a counting horse to attract people. The trainer asked the animal how many Gospels there are and the horse stamped his front, right hoof four times. How many commandments? The horse stamped ten times. How many apostles? The animal stamped twelve times. But when the trainer asked how many hypocrites were in the service that morning, the horse tap danced all over the front of the auditorium! The Jerusalem church resorted to no showy gimmicks. It kept its worship simple and basic, fresh and meaningful!

Want to be a New Testament church? Follow these examples from the practices of the Jerusalem congregation. Does your church measure up to that church in the way it loves? Does it match in the way it operates? Does it compare in the way it worships?

Chapter 3

The Magnificent Church
Antioch

THE FIRE-STORM OF PERSECUTION that flared up after Stephen's death drove the disciples out of Jerusalem. They scattered to Lebanon, Cyprus, and Syria. Some went as far as Antioch of Syria, preaching the gospel to gentiles. The people there received the gospel warmly and a great number turned to the Lord. When word of this came to Jerusalem, the church sent Barnabas to Antioch as a committee of one to check it out. He found it was truly a work of God. Instead of returning to Jerusalem to report, he stayed in Antioch to help.

So fast and so big grew the work that Barnabas could not handle it on his own. In the nearby city of Tarsus was Saul, the Jewish man who later became known by his Roman name Paul. The two men were well acquainted. It was Barnabas who met and welcomed Saul as a new believer in Jerusalem seven years before. Now he went to Tarsus and asked Saul to come and help in Antioch. Saul agreed. Under these two leaders, the work fairly exploded. Within a year, Antioch took its place alongside Jerusalem as a leading church (Acts 11:19–30).

Antioch was truly a "magnificent" New Testament church. But any church can share its magnificence and become a New Testament church like it.

EVANGELISTIC IN VISION

Saving a soul is God's work. Sharing the gospel is man's work. But when men do their part, God does his! When Christians from Cyprus and Cyrene hit town, they came "preaching the Lord Jesus" (Acts 11:20). "The hand of the Lord was with them; and a great number who believed turned to the Lord" (Acts 11:21). The ministries of Barnabas and Saul produced even more converts. "A great many people were added to the Lord" (Acts 11:24).

A young Presbyterian pastor said he believed God predestined some people to be saved and would save them without anybody's help. It appeared there were not many of these. Then he began aggressively sharing the gospel with a method the world now knows as Evangelism Explosion. "When I started sharing the gospel," said the pastor, "I was shocked at how many more people proved to be predestined!" To repeat: when men do their part, God does his!

This great growth in the number of disciples at Antioch did not happen just because folks there put up a red-brick building complete with stained-glass windows and a pipe organ, stuck a sign out front reading "The First Church of the Persecuted Followers of Jesus Christ, Incorporated. Traditional service at 11:00 a.m. Sunday; contemporary service at 7:00 p.m. Sunday," and rang chimes when it was time to meet. Antiochenes would have stayed away in droves! But when this church gave itself to aggressive evangelism, it changed the life of the whole city. In the first century, Antioch was devoted to pagan gods and sexual immorality. The Roman poet Juvenal said Antioch spewed its moral sewage into Rome, eventually corrupted that city, and destroyed the empire.[1] Maybe. But within three hundred years, half the population

---

1. Juvenal, "Satire 3."

of Antioch professed to follow Christ. If there was hope for Antioch, there is hope for any city.

This, I know: if ever a church becomes a magnificent New Testament church, evangelism must become its heartbeat. If a church gives up aggressive evangelism for maintenance ministries, if it settles for being a keeper of the aquarium rather than a fisher of men, if it loses its evangelistic zeal and the spirit of outreach and soul winning, God writes "Ichabod" ("the glory has departed") over its doors and takes away its lampstand (Rev 2:5)!

Does your church encourage people to share Christ? Does it train them for evangelism? Does your church practice evangelism? Is evangelism the main thing it does? Does your church have a plan to share the gospel with every person in the county? More personally, how long since you last made an effort to lead someone to Christ? How long since you prayed for a lost person? How long since you prayed with a lost person? To be a New Testament church, a congregation must prioritize evangelism.

GENEROUS IN GIVING

A prophet named Agabus came to town with a dark message. Soon a dire famine would hammer the whole Mediterranean world, especially Jerusalem. Already members of the mother church had impoverished themselves helping the needy after Pentecost. When this warning came, the church in Antioch immediately took up a love offering to help their poor brothers down in Judea (Acts 11:27–30). Antioch was not a rich church. In fact, the coming famine threatened them as well. But the members gave gladly, sacrificially, and generously to meet the needs of their distressed comrades in the mother church, a plight outside their local fellowship!

A farmer owned a prize Jersey cow. When a neighbor asked how much milk the cow gave, the farmer drawled, "Well, if you mean by way of voluntary contribution, she don't give nothing.

But if I can tie her horns so she can't hook, and her feet so she can't kick, I can squeeze about eleven quarts a day out of her!"[2]

No one had to squeeze money out of Antioch. Her members gave freely, by way of voluntary contribution. Every member helped with the offering. No names are given. The givers remained anonymous but generous. Its generosity made Antioch a magnificent New Testament church.

If any church ever becomes a magnificent New Testament church, it must develop the grace of generosity. A stingy church is not a magnificent church! It is not a New Testament church! How sad to see churches with big budgets giving so little to benevolence and to other believing communities in need.

Does your church give sacrificially to meet needs here and elsewhere? Is your church generous with other fellowships? How long since your church gave some support to a sister church with great needs? Has your church ever responded to needs created by a disaster? To be a New Testament church a congregation must be generous.

MISSIONARY IN HEART

On her front steps, there was a whole city to win, but Antioch kept an eye fixed on the regions beyond where the name of Jesus was yet to be heard. For them the Great Commission served as marching orders for the church. On its six "alls" this congregation had a firm grip: "all power," "all ye," "all the world," "all nations," "all things," and "all the days" (Matt 28:18–20 KJV)!

The Holy Spirit interrupted church one day with orders to set apart Barnabas and Saul for a special work. Five "prophets and teachers" worked in that congregation: Symeon Niger, Lucius, Manaen, Barnabas, and Saul. Barnabas and Saul were the best trained and most experienced of the five. But this "church that emptied its pockets of the money for the poor and needy also

2. Pierce, *Supreme Beatitude*, 17.

emptied its pulpit of its strongest and best men for the regions beyond" (Acts 13:1–3).[3] Antioch was magnificently mission-minded.

If any church ever becomes a magnificent New Testament church, it must become a world-class church with a global vision and a strong commitment to missions. A church expresses that vision and commitment both in money and in manpower. In a magnificent church, members talk about missions, but they do not just talk about missions. They pray for missions, but they do not just pray for missions. They give to missions, but they do not just give to missions. They do missions! To be a magnificent New Testament church, its members must not get so focused on the local scene that they forget there is a world out there to win to Jesus!

Does your church teach missions? Does it organize for missions? Does it plan missions? Does it budget for missions? Does it do missions? Does it hold the ropes for those who go down into the well of mission service? Does it earnestly pray that God will "send out" (Matt 9:38) its youth and children into missions? Does it give up its best leaders to the neediest fields?

Senti Yabang, from Nagaland, India, was a student of mine when I taught during a sabbatical at the Baptist Theological Seminary in Singapore. Out of genuine curiosity I asked him, "How did you become a Christian?"

"My parents were Christians."

"How did they become Christians?"

"My grandparents were Christians."

"How did they become Christians?"

"Your missionaries!" he said.

Then I learned that Nagaland and a couple of other Indian states in the northeast were between 90 and 95 percent Christian because of missionaries that toughed it out in the hard places in the world!

Senti asked me to thank American Christians for sending missionaries so his family could hear the gospel and be saved. Would it embarrass you if I gave his message directly to you? What have you given to support missions? Who did you send? What

3. McDaniel, *Churches*, 66.

have you done personally to get the gospel within the reach of the unreached? To be a New Testament church its members must be committed to missions.

ORTHODOX IN DOCTRINE

Certain men from Jerusalem came to Antioch insisting that a gentile first had to become a Jew, i.e., be circumcised and submit to the law of Moses (Acts 15:1), before he could accept the Jewish messiah Jesus. Together with Saul and Barnabas, the Antiochene church challenged these men and championed the gospel of salvation by grace alone through faith alone apart from works of any kind.

Since the Judaizers came from Jerusalem, to Jerusalem Antioch would go. In a meeting at the Holy City, the church at Antioch stood for free grace. When the dust settled, the conference agreed that salvation comes through faith alone and not by works, any works! Antioch stood firm on this doctrine and kept the faith. They defended the truth against heresy! They were magnificently orthodox in doctrine.

Do not misunderstand! At Antioch they did some new things but they kept believing the old things. Believers there were willing to try different approaches but they stayed solid and sound in their doctrine. A church can be progressive in methodology but a New Testament church must remain unflinchingly sound in theology.

Doctrine matters! In the 1980s, when the conservative resurgence hit the Southern Baptist Convention, strange words came from some denominational leaders. "We need to quit fighting over doctrine and get on with bold missions!" What? I am all for bold missions but the message matters! If the message does not matter, then Baptists should just send anyone willing to go. Maybe Baptists should give their money to the cults because they seem to do a better job! Perish the thought! The message matters! To be a New Testament church, its members must "contend for the faith that was once for all delivered to the saints" (Jude 3).

Does your church stand for the biblical faith? Does it hold to "the old-time religion"? Do the members care more about worship style than about the its core beliefs? Do they study doctrine? "How-to" series are good but does your church teach doctrine? Does it train youth and new members in the faith and practice of the New Testament? A magnificent New Testament church must be arrow-straight in doctrine, orthodox in theology.

I give you Antioch. Where can anyone find a more magnificent model for a New Testament church? Aggressive in evangelism! Generous in giving! Missionary in spirit! Orthodox in doctrine! So magnificent was this church that it soon caught the attention of the city. There was no good word to describe its members, so the citizens of Antioch made up one: "Christians" (Acts 11:26). It means "belonging to Christ." What a compliment! When the townsmen saw these disciples, they knew they belonged to Christ and so they called them by his name, "Christian."

What does your city think of your church? Do they believe its members deserve the name "Christian"? Live so as to earn that name! It will glorify the Lord Christ and go far toward making yours a New Testament church!

Chapter 4

The Matchless Church
Berea

AN IMPORTANT STAGING POST on the famous Roman road, the Via
Egnatia, Berea was forty-five miles west of Thessalonica and about
three hundred miles north of Athens. Paul planted a church there
on his second missionary tour. Gospel efforts in Thessalonica threw
the town into turmoil. To protect Paul and Silas from violence at
the hands of the Jews, Christians in the city sent the pair away se-
cretly. As was their custom, when they came to Berea, Paul and
Silas went first into the synagogue to preach. "To the Jew first and
also to the Greek" (Rom 1:16) remained the divine order. Berean
Jews were exceptional in that they did not prejudge the cause of
Christ but investigated it and found the evidence convincing. Many
came to Christ. Jews accepted Jesus as messiah. Greeks also saw the
light of Christ and came to him. Among the latter, Luke specifically
mentioned some "honorable women," apparently a few of the leading ladies in the city.

The work was going well at Berea until hostile Jews from
Thessalonica came to town, stirred the Jews into a fury, and made it
unsafe for Paul. Silas and Timothy were in no imminent danger, so
they stayed while the Christian brothers sent Paul the twenty-five

miles to the sea, and a group went with him by water to Athens. When they returned, they brought to Silas and Timothy a message from Paul: "Hurry and come to me!"

The story of Berea takes only six verses to tell (Acts 17:10–15), but the brief paragraph is rich with suggestions about how to make a matchless New Testament church.

RECEIVE THE WORD WITH GLADNESS

The Jews in Thessalonica were close-minded (Acts 17:1–9). They refused to listen. But those in Berea were more open-minded (Acts 17:11). In the original language, "open-minded" (*eugenesteros*) meant high-born, but it came to carry the more general idea of being open, tolerant, and generous, that is, of having the qualities that go with being well-born and bred. The open-minded Bereans were not only ready to listen but hungry to hear! In a matchless New Testament church, members listen eagerly and receive the word with readiness.

Seminaries try to teach preachers how to preach. In a preaching class at New Orleans Baptist Theological Seminary taught by Dr. Wilbur Schwartz it was my dear friend Wade Akins's turn to preach. He had prepared a sermon on Shamgar, an obscure character who is mentioned just twice in Judges. "After (Ehud) was Shamgar . . . who killed 600 Philistines with an ox goad" (Judg 3:31; 5:6). When it was their turn to preach in class, most students came in suits and ties. Akins showed up wearing an open neck dress shirt with sleeves rolled up above his elbows. He began his message imagining how Shamgar got up in the morning, dressed, and ate a big breakfast. Then he pictured how the man must have hugged and kissed his wife and each of his five or six children, then picked up his trusty ox goad, and went off to fight the Philistines. "I imagine he found a big rock, about as big as this 'pull-pit,' out in a field and hid behind it," continued Akins, crouching behind the pulpit to illustrate. The professor's assistant in the back was running a newfangled video camera and nearly went crazy because Akins had disappeared and the cameraman did not know where to aim his device. Akins went on: "Shamgar waited until he heard the Philistines riding in, 'biddy-bump, biddy-bump, biddy-bump.' When he could see the whites of their eyes, Shamgar jumped out from behind the rock." At that point, Akins leaped up from behind the pulpit. With great enthusiasm he acted out Shamgar's attack. "He took his trusty ox goad and hit them on the head, he hit them on the back, he hit them on the chest, he hit them on the legs. All day long he fought the enemy." Then Akins drew himself up, raised a fist and said dramatically, "And the Bible says he killed six hundred Philistines." Akins ended by making a few points about Shamgar's fight. When he finished, his hair was in his eyes, his right shirt sleeve had come unrolled and was flapping in the breeze, his shirttail was out, and he was walking on two inches of his pants legs!

By this time, the class was hysterical, but it got really quiet in the room when Dr. Schwartz made his way to the front. He paused for dramatic effect, looked over his glasses, and said, "Students, this demonstration just proves that all the ways to preach have not been tried yet!"

If preachers need to learn to preach (and they do), maybe congregations need to learn to listen! A man came down the aisle during an invitation and said to the pastor, "Please pray for my hearing." So the pastor laid his hands on the man's ears and prayed for God to open them. When the preacher finished, the fellow said, "Just a minute. You misunderstood. I meant I have a hearing before the local judge tomorrow!" Maybe we should pray for "hearing" because to be a New Testament church a congregation must know how to listen and gladly receive the word of God!

SEARCH THE SCRIPTURE TO VERIFY TEACHING

In Paul's day, the verb "search" was used in a legal sense to refer to the steps a lawyer took in examining and sifting evidence to see whether it would hold up in court. The Bereans did not take Paul's every word for granted. Each hearer had the right, indeed the duty, to investigate what the apostle said and to determine whether the inspired word of God backed it up. They wanted to make sure that what Paul was preaching was indeed the truth of God's Word.

Think of it: Paul was the most famous apostle and theologian of the early church. Yet the Bereans eagerly searched the sacred Scriptures to see if his teaching was truly biblical! They would not take Paul's word at face value but checked to see if the things he said were so. They wanted to know, "Is what this man says true? Was the crucified Nazarene really God in the flesh? And did he really rise from the dead? Is this what the Scriptures say about Messiah? Did the person, work, and suffering of Jesus of Nazareth fulfill the promises of the Old Testament? Let us search the Bible daily to find out whether these things are so."

Was it right for the Bereans to investigate Paul's teaching? One preacher out of Houston, Texas, thought they were out of line. In his opinion, "the Bereans were jackasses; they had no business checking up on the preacher." Why would he say that? Were they wrong to go to the Scriptures to evaluate the message Paul preached? Not at all! Why did that preacher say this about the Bereans? He said it because he wanted his people to blindly believe whatever he said! Listen, a man's teaching is not necessarily right just because he is on radio or television, or in a big church, or because of where he earned a degree, or where he teaches, or how many books he has published, or any other factor. He is right only if his teaching squares with the word of God.

It is Scripture, and Scripture alone, that is the final judge of all teaching. This is the Reformation principle of *sola scriptura*, "only Scripture." Scripture is the only authority for sinful man in seeking truth about God. *Sola scriptura* is foundational to Christianity. In the words of Reformer Martin Luther, the doctrine of *sola scriptura* means that "what is asserted without the Scriptures or proven revelation may be held as an opinion, but need not be believed."[1] Often in religious discussions people simply believe what a preacher or professor tells them. They ought rather to study God's word to

---

1. George, "Dr. Luther's Theology," 19.

confirm or dispute what is said. To be a New Testament church a congregation must check every message by the Scriptures!

PROTECT GOD'S SERVANTS FROM ATTACK

When the town turned against Paul, Berean Christians determined that no one would hurt him if they could prevent it. He had to get away, and they had to help him, but go he must. Trusted brothers took him to the coast and arranged passage on a ship at their expense. Some of them went with him all the way to Athens to make doubly sure no harm came to him (Acts 17:14–15). They would not rest until Paul was safe.

In a matchless New Testament church, the Berean spirit still lives. Around this country there are Berean-style believers who protect their pastor and other spiritual leaders. When the enemy comes in like a flood against God's servants, the members of a matchless New Testament church do not run, move their membership to some other church, or let the folks who are out to run off the pastor or staff member do their dirty work. They protect God's servants.

Fifty years ago a few members of the church I served as pastor decided it was time for me to move on. Their plan involved undermining my integrity. In a business meeting one of the group rose to the attack: "Some of us would like to know why the monthly long-distance telephone charges are always higher than the minimum?" she asked. Without ever directly accusing me of doing anything wrong, she implied ever so slyly that I used the church's long-distance phone service for personal calls (later I found out that this was the method this very group had used to run off the last six pastors before me).

When the woman asked her question and explained it, most of the members sat silently and spoke not a word. But a fellow on the pew just in front of her asked, "How much money are we talking about?"

"Thirteen dollars and twenty-seven cents," the church treasurer replied.

"Thirteen dollars and twenty-seven cents?" exclaimed the man. "Why, my wife and I run businesses out of our home and we think it is a great month when our phone bill is under two hundred dollars!" He stood up, turned to the woman who was pressing the accusation, pulled a twenty dollar bill out of his billfold and held it out to her. "If I give you twenty dollars, will you sit down and shut up and let the rest of us get on with God's business?" She turned the color of hawk meat, shut her mouth, sat down, and that was the end of it!

Had that man not been so ugly I would have kissed him right there. He and others like him swarmed to defend me. Because they did, I could have spent the rest of my life in that church. My ministry flourished and the work of the Lord prospered in that community because some folks there rose up to defend their pastor. To be a New Testament church a congregation must protect God's servants from attack!

Among the churches of the New Testament, Berea got no letter. It required none. A New Testament letter usually treated a problem or spoke of a danger. This is easy to see when it comes to other churches. Witness the backsliding in Galatia; the dim understanding of the spiritual unity of believers at Ephesus; the liberalism and license at Colossae; the enemies of the cross at Philippi; the idlers and busybodies at Thessalonica; the divisions and immorality at Corinth; and the tendency to pride at Rome. Consider also the subjects treated in Paul's letters to individuals: kindness to a slave in Philemon; false teaching in Timothy; human wisdom in Titus. Think about the conditions deplored and condemned in the letters by the two brothers of Jesus: fruitless faith in James; ungodly perversion of the common salvation in Jude. Look further at the five letters by apostles of Jesus that dealt with hopelessness in 1 Peter; false prophets in 2 Peter; false doctrine in 1 John; the Antichrist in 2 John; proud Diotrephes in 3 John. Check the letter to the Hebrews, challenging stunted babies in the church. But Berea got no letter because it did not need one. The Bereans boldly and consistently held the faith, lived the life, and worked the work.

Berea was a matchless New Testament church! May her tribe increase in the form of congregations eager to listen, faithful to check teaching by Scripture, and courageous to defend God's servants against attack!

Chapter 5

The Memorable Church
Ephesus

EPHESUS WAS UNFORGETTABLE. TOURISTS who visited the city came away with vivid mental images of it. In that day when trade followed river valleys, Ephesus stood on a good harbor at the mouth of the Cayster River, the largest and richest watershed in western Asia Minor. This made it a great trading and banking center. It served as capital of the Roman province of Asia. The Roman governor lived there and sometimes tried great cases of law in the city. From miles around, people came to Ephesus to the Pan-Ionian games that featured athletic events like those of the Olympics. The city was also a center of pagan superstition, famed for selling charms and spells guaranteed to ensure safety on a trip, to give children to the childless, and to secure success in love or business. At Ephesus was a twenty-four-thousand-seat theater, the largest outdoor venue in the ancient world. But Ephesus' crowning glory was the temple of Artemis (Diana), one of the Seven Wonders of the Ancient World. This building was 140 yards long, 75 yards wide, and had 127 pillars that were each 20 yards tall and the gift of a king. In it stood a many-breasted idol of a fertility goddess the Greeks called Artemis, an image so old no one knew where it came from. Legend said it fell from heaven as a gift of the gods (Acts 19:35).

Paul had good reasons to remember Ephesus. For him, it was a place of blood, sweat, and tears: the blood of conflict with beastly men (1 Cor 15:32); the sweat of labor to make a living for himself and his band of helpers; the tears of compassion for the lost he shed day and night (Acts 20:31, 34). He also remembered the city as the place where he did some of his finest work and had some of his best success. So great was the people's response to the gospel that the apostle spent nearly three years there, the longest he stayed at any one place on a mission tour (Acts 19:1–20; 20:31). For Paul, Ephesus was unforgettable.

The church at Ephesus had some remarkable characteristics. To be a memorable New Testament church, a congregation must match these marks.

OBEYING THE LORD

At Ephesus Paul found a dozen disciples of John the Baptist whom he could not recognize as genuine Christians. These men had heard John's call to repent as preparation for the coming of the messiah who would give the Holy Spirit. They submitted to John's baptism. So far, so good. But their spiritual experience did not go far enough and was not good enough.

"Did you receive the Holy Spirit *when* you believed?" asked Paul.[1] His question assumed the normal connection between believing and receiving the Spirit. Their answer was unsatisfactory: "We have not so much as heard whether the Holy Spirit was given" (Acts 19:2 KJV).[2] It was not his *existence* that was unknown to them; the Baptist had taught them about the Spirit. It was instead the Holy Spirit's *presence* about which this dozen was in the dark. When Paul filled them in on Pentecost, they received the Spirit and submitted to immersion in Jesus' name.

1. My emphasis added.

2. The phrase "was given" was added by the KJV translators, but reflects the probable meaning of the text.

These new believers might have balked at immersion. Many do! "Why, John already dunked us in the Jordan," they might have protested. "We have no need to be 'rebaptized.'" But they were not in the least hesitant or reluctant to obey the Lord's command (Acts 19:1–7). Eagerness to obey the Lord made the church at Ephesus memorable.

Eager obedience makes any church unforgettable! Multitudes call Jesus "Lord, Lord," but few do the things he said to do. Many never obey. Some who do, obey reluctantly or partially. Delayed obedience is instant disobedience. Partial obedience is total disobedience. But a congregation that obeys the Lord gladly and eagerly makes theirs a memorable church. In fact, it makes theirs a New Testament church.

I heard a story about General Robert E. Lee, commander in chief of the Confederate Army during the War Between the States, who sent word to General Stonewall Jackson that he wished to see him at Jackson's earliest convenience. General Jackson got the communiqué in the middle of the night. Immediately, he ordered his horse saddled and rode through a blinding snowstorm to the quarters of his commander. Lee was amazed and told Jackson that he had meant for him to come at his first convenience. As the story goes, Jackson replied with something like, "But, sir, your slightest wish is my supreme command!"

Is Jesus' slightest wish your supreme command? Does the Lord ever have to be careful what he tells you to do because he knows you will do it? How eager are you to do what Christ wants? To be a New Testament church a congregation must yield instant and complete obedience.

REACHING FOR THE UNREACHED

The work in Ephesus reached far beyond the city limits. Over the space of three years (Acts 20:31), "all the residents of Asia heard the word of the Lord, both Jews and Greeks" (Acts 19:8–10). The province of Asia included the whole western coast of modern Turkey and a huge part of the interior. Paul did not go out and evangelize it all by himself. In fact, he spent much of his time in Ephesus, making tents all morning and evening and teaching in the midday hours. The people of Asia Minor did not come in to town and crowd into the school of Tyrannus to hear Paul preach at noon. So how did the gospel spread? There was only one way. Believers from Ephesus penetrated every Asian district and city with the good news! Churches sprang up in Troas, Assos, Adramyttium, Miletus, Trogylleum, Hierapolis, Colossae, Smyrna, Pergamum, Sardis, Philadelphia, and Laodicea. In the history of Christian missions, there has never been a match for the zeal of Ephesian Christians in getting out the gospel and planting churches. Their heart for missions made this congregation a memorable New Testament church!

Great zeal for missions will make any church memorable! Does your church study much about missions? Study more! Does your church give much to missions? Give more! Does your church do much about missions? Do more! Take a fishing boat to a small island in Indonesia, or hack a path through the jungle in Peru, or climb over a mountain in China to take the gospel to a remote village where it has never gone before. Or lead a mission Vacation Bible School on the Colorado western slope, or on Manhattan Island, or in a nearby trailer park or apartment complex! To be a New Testament church a congregation must be zealous in missions.

DISPLAYING THE POWER OF GOD

To say that during Paul's years in Ephesus God moved with great power among the Ephesians (Acts 19:11–20) may be the understatement of the century! God worked "extraordinary miracles" through Paul. God healed the sick and cast out demons by means of "handkerchiefs" the apostle wore around his head to keep sweat out of his eyes and "aprons" he wore around his waist to hold his tools and protect his clothing while he worked. Just a touch from these garments and the sick recovered and evil spirits left the demonized.

Thousands were converted, including such notable citizens as Tychichus, Epaphras, Philemon, and Trophimus. Idolaters turned to Christ from Artemis in such numbers that her famed temple was nearly deserted. By droves, Ephesians abandoned the black arts of witchcraft and sorcery and magic. New Christians brought their expensive, hand-copied books full of incantations and spells and burned them publicly in the original bonfire of the vanities. The books' value came to fifty thousand drachmas (one drachma was a fair day's wage) or about 137 years of continuous labor.

Business got so bad for the silversmiths who made small images of Artemis to sell to visitors that they organized a two-hour protest in the city theater and ran Paul out of town. In short, the true and living God challenged the dark lord and crushed him so badly his followers could not stand it!

The gospel spread and triumphed until it turned the whole city right side up! It put God's power on display! Hard hearts were softened and closed minds opened. Sin's shackles were broken and the dark lord ripped from his throne. God's power came down in amazing ways! No wonder the church at Ephesus was unforgettable!

A church must never lose its grip on gospel truth. But a New Testament church must never forget that the gospel is more than just truth. It is "the power of God for salvation" (Rom 1:16)! Elisha cried, "Where is the Lord God of Elijah?" (2 Kgs 2:14). I ask, Where is the Lord God of Ephesus? Where is the God of power and burning? Where is the God of miracle and might? To experience the power of God makes any church memorable.

A young pastor invited an older minister to come and hold a "quiet hour" in his church. The older man declined, saying, "What your church needs is not a quiet hour but an earthquake!" I long for an earthquake when the power of God falls! And I live with the fear my children and grandchildren will never know what it looks like when the power of God shakes a place.

To be a New Testament church a congregation must display God's power at work. I give you the church at Ephesus. Resolve to become more like it! Is there some place you need to begin to obey God? Has God put missions on your heart? Do you earnestly pray for God's power to fall in your church? To match Ephesus is to become what the Lord Jesus means every church to be. It is, in fact, to become a New Testament church!

Chapter 6

The Munificent Church
Philippi

TWICE THE HOLY SPIRIT forbade Paul to preach any more in Asia
Minor (Acts 16:6–7). As sensitive as a compass needle to the North
Pole, he followed the Spirit's leading to ancient Troy on the Aegean
Sea. There in a vision in the night Paul saw a man on the Macedonian shore begging, "Come over . . . and help us!" It was Europe's
cry for the gospel! Athens, crowded with countless gods! Corinth,
jaded by wine, women, and song. Thessalonica and Berea, where
Jews and God-fearing Greeks longed for the hope of Israel. Dio-
nysius and Damaris, wanting something better than the empty
philosophies of the Stoics and Epicureans. Lydia, hungry for a
glory greater than her royal purple goods. A wretched fortune-
teller, desperate to be free from an evil spirit. All these stood up
in the form of a single man and joined their voices in a piercing
cry for help that rang across the wine-dark sea. Ever obedient to
a heavenly vision, Paul straightway sailed to Europe and made for
Philippi (Acts 16:8–10).

One sabbath evening, soon after they arrived, Paul and his
friends looked for a synagogue but found none in that city. Judaism
was too feeble there to support a synagogue. It took only ten males

to form one but the Jewish men in Philippi had no faith or interest. However, some women (God bless them!) kept prayer meeting going. Paul found a group gathered beside the river Gangites, about a mile west of the city. The apostle sat down and preached Jesus to them. Among the women was Lydia from Thyatira in Asia Minor. She and some of her servants were in Philippi on business, either buying or selling purple dye or purple cloth. As Paul preached, "the Lord opened her heart" and she became a believer. So began the church at Philippi, the first on European soil (Acts 16:11–15).

The congregation at Philippi deserves fame for its munificence. Three references point out the great causes they gave to so lavishly.

MINISTERS

At Philippi, Paul started something new. To this point he had supported himself fully by making tents. Most rabbis learned and practiced a trade so they could teach without charge. But Paul made no tents while he worked for the Lord at Philippi. Instead, the people who responded to his preaching took care of him and his party of at least three, including Silas, Timothy, and Luke. Lydia invited Paul and his team to use her house as their base while they worked in the city. They accepted her offer. Such provision left Paul and his group free to give full attention to spiritual things (Acts 16:9–15). From the first day, the Philippians generously supported the preachers of the gospel in their local work.

Much praise belongs to ministers who "make tents" to earn a living so they can preach the gospel of Christ. But more praise belongs to those churches who relieve their ministers from the need to make a living. The Bible says, "Those who preach the gospel should live of the gospel" (1 Cor 9:14 KJV). That phrase means, not that a preacher should practice what he preaches (although he certainly should) but that a preacher has a right to draw financial support from those to whom he ministers spiritually. Some churches are generous with everyone and everything but its ministers.

President Woodrow Wilson's father was a Presbyterian pastor. One day Rev. Wilson drove up to the little general store in his town in a shiny buggy drawn by a sleek horse. Some of his church members standing there noted that the pastor's clothes were worn and frayed. One said, "Preacher, your horse and buggy look better than you do!"

"There is a good reason for that, my man," said Rev. Wilson. "You see, I take care of my horse and buggy but my church takes care of me!"[1]

I knew a church that used to brag about giving more than 30 percent of its annual income through its denominational missions program but kept its pastor living near poverty level for more than thirty years. That is just plain wrong! It is certainly not the mark of a New Testament church.

The Philippians generously supported those who ministered spiritually among them! At a former church, a member of the finance committee, discussing my compensation, said, "You know, if you add in the parsonage, you make about what I bring home from my job!" He made two errors. First, the church was not giving me the house. I owned not one cent of equity in it. Second, take-home pay and gross pay are two entirely different things. He was looking at money he brought home after taxes, health insurance, and other deductions. It was about the same as my gross pay, out of which I paid my own taxes, health insurance, and retirement. It is wrong to compare take-home pay to the total support offered a minister by a church. The question about preacher-pay is not "Is that enough?" but "Is this generous?" To be a New Testament church a congregation must support its ministers generously!

MISSIONS

At Philippi, the church also started something new. When Paul left town to continue his mission work elsewhere, they sent offerings to him. "Partnership" (*koinonia*) includes financial sharing. Their

---

1. Grey, "Pastor."

support freed Paul from spending valuable time making tents to make ends meet while he did mission work. Paul wrote this very letter to thank the Philippians for one such love gift, although clearly they sent gifts more than once (Phil 4:15–18). This congregation was the first, and for some time the only, church to support Paul's bold mission thrust.

A great sin of modern churches is selfishness. It is selfish for the average Southern Baptist church to keep up to ninety cents of every dollar given (and some keep more) for their own local use. Some of the largest churches in the Southern Baptist Convention give only 2 to 3 percent of receipts through the denomination's missions program. The pastors of those churches say, "Yes, the percentage is low but look at the number of dollars!" However, not one of those pastors would let a wealthy member use that argument to excuse himself from tithing! It is selfish for a church to spend seven times as much on buildings and properties every year as it gives to all mission efforts combined. It is selfish for a church to spend more every year just to pay interest on loans for land and buildings than it gives to all mission causes combined!

The Philippians supported missions generously. Does your church budget generously for missions? Does it set challenging goals for mission offerings and exceed them? Does it give generously to help those who go? I long to see the day that every church gives half of all budget receipts to missions and evangelism. I pray for the day when every member of every church gives at least one dollar more to special missions' offerings than they spend on Christmas presents for other people on Jesus' birthday! That is the Philippian spirit! To be a New Testament church a congregation must give generously to missions.

NEEDS

Hard times had "come a'knockin'" at the doors of Christians in Jerusalem. Many of them had impoverished themselves to take care of the new converts from every nation who stayed in the city after Pentecost to learn about their new-found faith. Not long after, during the reign of Claudius Caesar (AD 41–50), a famine swept the eastern Mediterranean and added to the distress of the Jerusalem Christians. In that distress, Paul saw a great opportunity to bring together the gentile and Jewish wings of the church. So he went to the largely gentile churches he founded and asked them to raise a love offering to aid their Jerusalem brothers. Instructions for this offering he gave to the Corinthian Christians in 1 Cor 16. The Corinthians made a start on this offering, but a year or so passed with little progress made. To encourage them, Paul lifted up the Macedonian churches as models. Among these congregations in Macedonia were the Bereans, the Thessalonians, and the Philippians, all of whom gave generously to feed, clothe, and house poor Christians in Jerusalem (2 Cor 8:1–5).

To this offering, the Philippians gave sacrificially (2 Cor 8:3). They themselves were poor, partly because their Roman conquerors had exploited their rich natural resources and partly because a series of Roman civil wars had been fought on their land. But along with the other Macedonian congregations, the Philippians stepped forward to help meet the needs in Jerusalem. Also, they gave voluntarily, "of their own accord" (2 Cor 8:3). No one pushed them. When the needs were pointed out, they gave. And the Philippians gave insistently. They actually pled "for the favor of taking part in the relief of the saints" (2 Cor 8:4). No one had to beg them to give; they begged to be allowed to give! Let their tribe increase!

Philippi gave generously to aid men and women in distress wherever they were, whether the need was local or in some far-flung corner of the world. How does your church respond to disasters? What does it do to feed, clothe, and house the poor? How does your church care for unwed mothers and unwanted children? What does it do to provide for widows and orphans? How does your church help those enslaved in the sex trade or in drug addiction? What does it do to provide clean water and food for people who have access to neither?

To be a New Testament church, a congregation must give generously to meet needs here, there, and everywhere. The generosity of any church is limited by the generosity of its members! No church can give generously for anything unless its members first give generously to their church!

One Baptist brother printed up a business card that read as follows:

> Reverend Doctor James Ebenezer Jackson, Junior, Pastor.
> Second Greater Downtown New Saint James Baptist Church.
> Sunday services at 11:00 a.m. and 7:00 p.m.
> In the work of the gospel, three books are necessary: the Bible book, the hymnbook, and the pocketbook.
> Come Sunday and open all three!

If any church is to be a New Testament church, members must come on Sunday with the Bible book, the hymnbook, and the pocket book. And open all three!

Is your church generous? It can be generous only if its members are generous! In the United States, average giving to all church causes totals only 4.35 percent of average income.[2] Be generous. Increase your giving. If you give a set amount, up that amount by 1 percent. If you give a tithe (10 percent) or more, up that amount an additional 1 percent.

2. Nieuwhof, "Church Giving Statistics."

Chapter 7

The Model Church
Thessalonica

PAUL AND SILAS PLANTED the church in Thessalonica (Acts 17:1–9). As was his custom, Paul began by preaching in the local synagogue to God's ancient people. This complies with the divine order, "to the Jew first, and also to the Greek" (Rom 1:16). Paul's message was that Jesus of Nazareth was God's messiah. From the first, the death of Jesus was a major obstacle that kept Jews from accepting him as the Christ of God. They looked for a messiah who would be a king like David at his best. At his best, David won all his battles. So, if the messiah lost even one battle, it proved he was not the messiah. No crucified messiah for them!

Paul met their objection head on! Over a period of three weeks he spoke to the Jews, explaining to them from the Hebrew Bible (e.g., Isa 53; Ps 22) that it was necessary for the messiah to suffer and die. Paul won some converts among the Thessalonian Jews, the "God fearers," i.e., gentiles who worshiped the God of Israel but refused to become full proselytes, and some prominent women of the city. Despite this good beginning, it did not take long for persecution to break out. Unbelieving Jews drove Paul from the synagogue and eventually from the city.

Taken alone, the Acts passage might suggest that Paul and his party stayed only a few weeks in Thessalonica, but there are hints of a longer period. There was enough time for "a great many of the devout Greeks and not a few of the leading women" (Acts 17:4) to become believers. Also, Paul reminded the Philippians that, during his stay at Thessalonica, they sent him help at least twice (Phil 4:15–16). These facts suggests a stay of significant length.

There is no record of the number of members, the kinds of ministries they exercised, where they gathered, or who led them. But in his first letter to the Thessalonian believers, Paul referred to them as an "example to all the believers in Macedonia and in Achaia" (1 Thess 1:7), i.e., all of Greece. This was a model church!

Take care with that word "model." I heard of a pastor who once said his people called him a model pastor. He took a lot of pride in that until one day he checked the dictionary definition of "model." It said a model was "a small imitation of the real thing!" But Paul meant the church at Thessalonica set some good patterns to follow.

WORK

When Paul thought about the Thessalonians, he remembered their "work of faith and labor of love and steadfastness of hope," and how they "turned to God from idols, to serve the living and true God" (1 Thess 1:2–3, 9). Members there understood that they were saved to serve, not to sit! So this church was working and laboring and patiently looking to God for the results. Some Christians work like I used to fish. I kept my hook in the water for only a little while. Unless I caught some fish quickly, I lost "the patience of hope" and quit. Not so the people of God at Thessalonica. They did not grow weary in well-doing! Small results did not dishearten them. Results were up to the Lord! They just put their hands to the work and never quit.

Thessalonian Christians would not recognize the current weak and sickly generation of Christians. Most are Jehovah's bystanders. They want no responsibility. It is about all they can do to drag themselves to church on an occasional Sunday morning and hold on to the back of the pew in front of them to stand while they murmur, "Oh, land of rest, for thee I sigh!" Most want programs that produce results without effort, visitation programs that bring in people without visiting, and baptisms without knocking on doors in search of the lost. They adopt programs from churches in Illinois or California and then sit back waiting for the same success those churches have but without hitting a lick of work! One year, North Phoenix Baptist Church won and baptized over five hundred people. Folks came from everywhere to find the secret to such success. Then-pastor Richard Jackson said, "There is no secret. Any church can baptize over five hundred in a year if they have six hundred men going out with the gospel every Monday night!"

How shameful that churches have to settle for nothing more than warm bodies in key jobs. The only way some folks will take a job is if the nominating committee promises, "It won't be much work."

A pastor search committee from an East Texas town once asked me, "Preacher, how will you motivate us to do what we know we should be doing?" I had a few ideas about how to do that, but their real problem was a failure of "faith, love and hope!" The Thessalonians worked because they had faith, love, and hope; those Texans did not work because they lacked all three.

It is not exactly clear what kind of work the Thessalonians did. Maybe it is best not to know. They just did what needed to be done. There is plenty to do! What on earth are you doing for heaven's sake? To be a New Testament church a congregation must have callouses from doing the Lord's work.

JOY

"You received the word in much affliction, with the joy of the Holy Spirit" (1 Thess 1:6). As soon as Thessalonians became Christians, enemies of the gospel attacked. Unbelieving Jews gathered a band of base fellows, stirred the city into an uproar, surrounded the house of Jason where the missionaries had been staying, and demanded that he hand over Paul, Silas, and Timothy. When the mob discovered the trio was not there, they hauled Jason and all the believers they could find before the rulers of the city, crying, "These men that have turned the world upside down have come here also" (Acts 17:5–6).

Faithfulness makes foes for at least two reasons. First, by its very nature righteousness is confrontational. If a man does right, it irritates those who do wrong because he makes them look bad in comparison. Second, following Jesus antagonizes the world because it turns the world right side up. To people standing on their heads instead of their feet, this makes the world look upside down. This, they cannot stand.

Jesus put it this way: "If the world hates you, know that it has hated me before it hated you. . . . If they persecuted me, they will also persecute you" (John 15:18, 20). He added, "Woe to you, when all people speak well of you" (Luke 6:26). It is not a Christian's job to be popular. It is his job to be faithful, even if faithfulness breeds hatred and leads to persecution!

Many followers of Jesus endure suffering poorly, griping, groaning, and complaining at every step. Yet even in suffering the Thessalonian Christians were filled with a strange joy, the fruit of the Spirit! The Spirit brought unutterable joy when the people had no reason to be happy! But even when hurt, mistreated, and criticized, the Thessalonians rejoiced with "joy that is inexpressible and filled with glory!" (1 Pet 1:8).

Members of a model New Testament church rejoice even in pain. Is your church a joyful people? Is your congregation joyful when they sing? In a worship service a few years ago my eight- and five-year-old granddaughters held hands and danced in a circle during one song. After church more than one member remarked, "I wish we would all do that!" Do you have joy in your heart and a smile on your lips? Do you rejoice to hear the word? When you give, are you a cheerful giver? To be a New Testament church, a congregation must rejoice. "And again I say, Rejoice! (Phil 4:4 KJV).

WITNESS

"Not only has the word of the Lord sounded forth from you in Macedonia and Achaia, but your faith in God has gone forth everywhere, so that we need not say anything" (1 Thess 1:7–8). Their witness in deed and in word was widely known!

The difference the gospel made in their lives soon had the whole province talking. Crooked men became straight. Liars became truth-tellers. Drunks became sober. Parents who never cared for their children became family-oriented. People with dirty mouths became decent. Sexually promiscuous people became pure. And the city noticed! The way Christians lived was a witness. People come and go past many a church and never notice the people at all. Not at Thessalonica. They lived the gospel. No one could ignore them.

The Thessalonians also spoke the gospel. In the original language of the New Testament, "sounded out" meant "to sound out" like a trumpet. They verbalized their witness.

A vice president at the university where I taught once said to me, "I just let my life be my witness."

I replied, "I hope you realize that is a cop-out! First, your claim reflects unbelievable arrogance. No one lives such a good and godly life that people crowd around asking, 'What makes the difference in your life?' If you can look at someone and tell whether that person is a Christian, come with me to the bus station downtown and point out the believers as the people get off the buses. You cannot. Second, without a verbal witness a good life is nothing more than an uninterpreted parable. People may see your faith in action, but they will never know Jesus made the difference unless you tell them!" She did not like what I said, but it was the truth!

To be a New Testament church a congregation must let people see the gospel in deed, but also make sure they hear it in word!

WATCH

Of the Thessalonian Christians, Paul wrote that they "wait for his Son from heaven, whom he raised from the dead, Jesus who delivers us from the wrath to come" (1 Thess 1:10). They lived in the hope of the second coming and final deliverance from the wrath of hell. Paul's letters show they did not have all the details straight. Events surrounding the coming of the Lord were for them "a riddle wrapped in a mystery inside an enigma."[1] But they did not have to get all the details right. Paul taught them to look for Jesus, not all the things surrounding his return! They waited expectantly for the Lord himself!

On a stone platform facing Tokyo's Shibuya rail station, the third largest station on the city lines, sits a bronze statue of a dog named Hachiko. The canine was an Akita, a large breed native to the mountains of northern Japan, who belonged to Dr. Ueno, a professor of agriculture at the Japanese Imperial University. Ueno got the dog in 1923 when it was just a puppy. For several months, Hachiko went with his master to Shibuya station every morning when Ueno left for work, and when the professor returned on the 6:00 p.m. train, the dog was waiting for him at the station.

On May 21, 1925, when Hachiko was eighteen months old, he went to the train station at 6:00 p.m. to meet his master. But the professor never came home that day. In fact, he never came home again. Ueno suffered a cerebral hemorrhage at work and died instantly. But every day for the next nine years, Hachiko went back to the station to meet the 6:00 p.m. train he thought would bring his beloved master home. This daily vigil at the station he kept until he died in 1935. If dogs think, surely Hachiko thought, "Master did not come home yesterday or the day before, but this may be the day!" Every day he went to Shibuya station to watch and wait for his master.

Whenever Jesus comes, noon or midnight, today or tomorrow, he should find his disciples watching for him as faithfully as Hachiko watched for his master! Members of a New Testament

---

1. International Churchill Society, "Russia."

church never lay their heads on a pillow at night without thinking that, maybe before day dawns, the "final morning" will break. They never start a day's work without thinking that perhaps the Lord will interrupt their work and begin his own. Blessed are those whom the Lord finds watching!

To be a New Testament church a congregation must keep its eyes fixed on the skies waiting for the Lord's return! The church at Thessalonica provides a challenging model for modern congregations who want to be like the churches of the New Testament. Work! Rejoice! Witness! Watch! Putting that pattern in place will benefit any congregation and actually move it toward being a New Testament church.

Chapter 8

The Muddled Church
Corinth

WITH A POPULATION OF perhaps five hundred thousand, Corinth was the largest and most prosperous city in Greece and served as the capital of Achaia. Located on the isthmus that linked northern Greece with the Peloponnesian peninsula, it had two seaports: Cenchrea to the east on the Aegean Sea and Lechaeum to the west on the Gulf of Corinth. Ships docked at one port, off-loaded cargo, and often were hauled along the *Diolkos*, a paved overland pathway, to the other side where they were reloaded and sailed on. Every two years Corinth hosted the Isthmian Games, from which Paul may have drawn the athletic language he used in his letters.

Such a moral cesspool was first-century Corinth that the name of the city was synonymous with an immoral lifestyle and even gave rise to a verb—"to corinthianize"—that meant to corrupt someone. To call someone a "Corinthian" was to imply that he had no morals!

Paul first came to Corinth near the end of his second missionary trip (Acts 18:1–18). He roomed with Priscilla and Aquila. After an eighteen-month ministry planting a church in that city (or churches in the area), he returned to his home base, Antioch of

Syria. On his third missionary trip, he spent three years in Ephesus (Acts 20:31), during which he picked up the thread of contact with the Corinthians, which can be summarized as follows.

1. In 1 Cor 5:9, Paul mentioned a previous letter to this congregation in which he warned believers not to keep company with immoral people. They mistakenly took him to mean they should have no contact at all with non-Christians (1 Cor 5:9–11).

2. At Ephesus, Paul heard from Corinth. The people sent a letter (1 Cor 7:1) asking about certain issues troubling the church, and the messengers who brought the letter added information about other problems with division and ugly sex sin (1 Cor 1:11–12; 16:15–18). In answer, Paul wrote 1 Corinthians and sent Timothy to deliver it (1 Cor 4:17). This letter shows just how muddled the church was. They had critical issues and numerous questions, but no answers. Paul gave them answers and directives in "words . . . taught by the Holy Spirit" (1 Cor 2:13).

3. First Corinthians did not solve the problems. Instead, the situation grew worse, so Paul made an unscheduled and unannounced trip to Corinth to set things in order. Acts does not mention this visit but the evidence appears in Paul's second letter to them. If he spoke of coming to them for a third visit (2 Cor 12:14; 13:1–2), he must have made a second visit after his first trip when he founded the church. This third trip proved to be a painful visit (2 Cor 2:1) because on it he was humbled and grieved (2 Cor 12:21). An unidentified person Paul tried to rebuke defied the apostle's authority and attacked him publicly (2 Cor 2:5; 7:12). Apparently the congregation entered a conspiracy of silence by not defending Paul (2 Cor 2:3), so he withdrew.

4. Back in Ephesus and deeply hurt, Paul wrote a painful letter over which he shed "many tears" (2 Cor 2:1–4) and with which he meant to straighten out the problems at Corinth. It grieved the church greatly, and Paul later admitted that

he regretted sending it (2 Cor 7:8). His description of this missive (2 Cor 7:8–13) fits neither the letter referred to in 1 Cor 5:9, nor 1 Corinthians itself. Apparently it was a separate letter, probably delivered by Titus (2 Cor 7:6–7), that did not survive.

5. Paul planned to meet Titus in Troas (2 Cor 2:12–13) but was so anxious for word from Corinth that he set out to find Titus along the way. When they met, Titus brought good news. The letter had won back the majority. The church had disciplined the defiant individual. Discipline broke his arrogance and he repented. Paul wrote 2 Corinthians to express his relief, to urge the congregation to restore the repentant man, and to deal with a new threat posed by false apostles (who may have been behind the defiant man). This epistle Paul sent with Titus back to Corinth with word that the apostle himself would follow soon (2 Cor 13:1–4; Acts 20:2).

6. Later, Paul probably wintered at Corinth before traveling to Jerusalem with the group taking the collection to the poor believers there (1 Cor 16:5–7).

In the Corinthian correspondence, Paul focused on the problems the Corinthian congregation faced and the questions they raised instead of highlighting characteristics that showed them as good examples. That poses a huge problem for anyone looking for positive patterns contemporary congregations should employ to be an authentic New Testament church. In both letters, Paul sent clear corrective messages to this troubled church. Did they follow his directives? No one knows for sure. Perhaps they did. Perhaps not. But, if they did as he told them to do, they would have provided some good models for the making of a New Testament church. That is the reason for including this church here. Had they corrected their problems, the church at Corinth would provide at least the following patterns important to forming a New Testament church.

STRESS UNITY OVER INDIVIDUAL PREFERENCES

The Corinthian congregation had two huge problems they failed to mention in the list of questions they sent to Paul. That is not unusual. Over my years at the University of Mobile, I made it a point to caution ministry students that search committees usually never tell prospective pastors about their church's biggest problems. Ministers have to discover those on their own!

The first problem Paul learned about came from the people who delivered the letter to him. There was division and quarreling in the church (1 Cor 1:10–17), centering on spiritual leaders. The fellowship fractured into four factions. One group claimed to follow eloquent Apollos; a second postured as partisans of Peter; a third preferred simple and plain-spoken Paul; and a fourth, maybe the fiercest competitors of all, just said, "We are Christ's party!" The congregation divided over what could be called "preacher preference." Regardless of the issue over which they quarrel, division will destroy any church. So the apostle appealed for unity over individual preferences. "Is Christ divided up among you? Was I crucified for you? Did I baptize you?" The questions demand negative answers (although Paul did baptize the house of Stephanas, according to 1 Cor 1:16). Rivalries based on personal preferences are childish, unspiritual, and terribly destructive.

This demand for unity has gone unheeded in many corners of the Christian world. Churches are crippled, and some have died in wars over worship styles. Many have to offer services offering contemporary worship as well as services featuring more traditional worship to suit their members' preferences. Somewhere along the way, a lot of Christians have lost sight of the fundamental truth that worship is not about them but about him, the Lord Jesus! Similar divisions often occur over preacher styles. Some members like Rev. A; others prefer Rev. B; and still others cannot be satisfied without Rev. C. Again, personal preferences too often trump Christian unity.

Had Corinth heard and heeded Paul's directive on this matter, she would stand as an example of choosing Christian unity over personal preference, a great pattern for a New Testament church.

EXERCISE CHURCH DISCIPLINE

A second matter also did not make the formal list sent to Paul. It was reported to him by the group from Corinth that delivered the letter of questions. There was gross sin in the church (1 Cor 5:1–12). One of their members was involved in an immoral sexual affair with "his father's wife," apparently his stepmother and not "his mother." This woman does not appear to have been a believer or a church member because no penalty is prescribed for her. Paul rebuked the congregation for tolerating a member engaged in such sinful behavior and ordered them to excommunicate him. "You are to deliver this man to Satan for the destruction of the flesh, so that his spirit may be saved in the day of the Lord" (1 Cor 5:5). The apostle's language suggests this man's sexual immorality may fit into the category of "sin that leads to death" (1 John 5:16), not eternal death but the loss of physical life! Discipline must be carried out not only for the sake of the sinner but also for the sake of the congregation, i.e., to keep his sin from spreading like leaven to others (1 Cor 5:6–7a). Note that this expulsion was to be the action of the congregation "when you are assembled in the name of the Lord Jesus" (1 Cor 5:4), not carried out by the pastoral staff or deacons alone. This means that church membership was a feature of Christian life from the first because there had to be an identifiable body of believers from which the sexually immoral member could be expelled and which formed the group that removed him from membership.

Happily, the Corinthians heeded this word from Paul and excommunicated the man in question. It humbled him and led to his repentance. When he repented, Paul commended the church for quickly and lovingly restoring him to fellowship (2 Cor 2:5–11).

Not one in a thousand churches practices church discipline, even for glaring public sins. Although most admit it is a biblical practice, few have ever disciplined even a single member and most have never given a single thought about a procedure to follow. Corinth learned her lesson about discipline, so it is fitting that she provides a profile here for New Testament churches to follow!

SETTLE DISPUTES BETWEEN FELLOW BELIEVERS

Some think the problem of lawsuits (1 Cor 6:1–8) may be tied to the problem with the immoral church member because Paul's discussion of them occurs in the middle of his rebuke of that man. No one knows for sure. However, the apostle clearly opposed a brother going to court against a brother, especially before unbelievers (1 Cor 6:6). Disputes should be handled, not by the "unrighteous" but by the "saints" (1 Cor 6:1), i.e., other Christians. The church court outranks every world court, including the Supreme Court of the United States. If the saints of God will judge "the world" and even "angels," as Paul argued, surely they are capable of settling issues between Christian brothers (1 Cor 6:5). If no satisfactory solution emerges from an attempt at arbitration, the apostle ordered wronged brothers to suffer being defrauded (1 Cor 6:7) rather than to go to court and expose Christ and his church to public ridicule.

Most churches are not prepared for this kind of action. They have no policies to guide them, no proposal to study the matter, and no plan ever to put such a program in motion. In recent years, a professing Christian cheated me out of a lot of money. He needed thirty thousand dollars quickly and could not access it soon enough, so my wife and I lent him twenty thousand dollars, which he promised to repay. The fellow made three, one thousand dollar payments, then never paid another penny. After over a year, following what I understand Paul to have ordered here, I asked the man's pastor if he would convene a council to hear the complaint and lead us to a binding arbitration. He declined, saying his church had no procedures to govern such an action and, further, no plans to produce any. In fact, when I asked how I should handle the matter, he told me to sue! Clearly that is the one thing Paul said a Christian was not to do to another believer. I had no recourse but to accept being defrauded by a professed Christian brother.

Did the Corinthians follow Paul's instruction and handle problems and issues between Christian brothers? No one knows. However, any congregation that wants to be a New Testament church should hear and heed God's word through the apostle and gear up to resolve conflicts, disputes, and disagreements between its members and even between its members and Christians belonging to other congregations.

LIVE CLEAN IN A FILTHY CULTURE

That Corinth was a terrible place to live is beyond question. In the ancient world, Corinth was considered one of the most immoral cities around. In classical times, the temple of Aphrodite on the Acrocorinth employed at least a thousand sacred prostitutes in its worship. It is not certain this continued into the Roman period, but it probably did. Also, Corinth was a port city, through which passed the basest of persons. Sailors often earned their reputation for having women in every port! The city won fame for its moral corruption. A "Corinthian girl" was a common word for a prostitute. A *korinthiastes*, properly a businessman, came to mean a "pimp." So "to live like a Corinthian" meant to practice sexual immorality. This was simply a way of life in the ancient world, but Corinth outdid most other cities in its wickedness.

Paul called the Corinthian Christians to live pure lives in that sin-saturated city. "Flee from sexual immorality" (1 Cor 6:18) and do not indulge in it (1 Cor 10:8). "Let us cleanse ourselves from every defilement of body and spirit" (2 Cor 7:1). Did the Corinthians obey his orders? No one knows for sure. But if they did, they would qualify as a pattern-setter for New Testament churches.

In what all too often becomes a misguided effort to be "seeker friendly," too many congregations now soft-pedal biblical morality and say little or nothing about it. They accommodate to the spiritual darkness of their surroundings as Lot did in Sodom (Gen 19). Members pay little attention to the moral demands of the

Bible. It is hard to distinguish believers from unbelievers by looking at their lifestyles. To be a New Testament church, however, a congregation must never compromise on biblical morality and its members must live pure, shining as diamonds on black velvet and upholding the moral demands of the Lord.

MEET THE NEEDS OF OTHER CHRISTIANS AND CHURCHES

Christianity is not a "Lone Ranger" religion. It entails consideration for other believers and even for other congregations. Paul urged the Corinthians to care for the "weak" among them. The specific issue he addressed was the eating of meat that had been sacrificed to idols (1 Cor 8:1—11:1). In the ancient world pagan temples were the main suppliers of meat for butcher shops. The priests took the cuts necessary for the sacrifices, ate some of the rest, and sold the remainder in markets known as "shambles." Observant Jews usually bought meat in kosher shops to avoid meat from pagan sacrifices. Must Christians be as scrupulous as the Jews? Paul advocated freedom to eat, because idols are nothing. But he cautioned that to eat, knowing it wounded brothers with weaker consciences, was wrong (1 Cor 8:1–13). Liberty has parameters set by concern for the spiritual welfare of other Christians.

Did the Corinthians follow his injunction? No one knows. But, if they did, they would have provided an important pattern for a New Testament church. No one should insist on his personal Christian liberty if it throws a stumbling block in the path of other brothers.

Also, Paul enlisted the Corinthian church in his campaign to raise funds to help needy Christians at Jerusalem (1 Cor 16:1–3). What was the problem? Most early Christians came from poorer classes who owned very little to begin with. Jews from many nations crowded into Jerusalem for Pentecost. The thousands of converts needed instruction in their new-found faith in Jesus as Messiah but had not prepared for an extended stay in the city. So Jerusalem Christians who had real property sold it and pooled the money to care for these guests (Acts 4:34–37). Then, when a famine struck the Mediterranean world just a few years later, it was disastrous. These Christians had absolutely nothing to fall back on. They were in dire straits.

With great enthusiasm, the Corinthian church agreed to join other congregations in gathering a love offering for their suffering brothers there. A year later, however, they had made little progress. Other churches had gone forward with their love offering, but not the Corinthians. So Paul challenged them to carry out their commitment to help that ailing congregation in Jerusalem (2 Cor 8:10–11).

Did they? It seems they did (2 Cor 9:1–2), but no precise details are available. If they did, it would set a pattern for congregations that want to be New Testament churches. Competition for people and dollars keeps most congregations self-centered. Some churches discourage their youth from going to a youth function sponsored by a different congregation because they fear they will lose their youth to that congregation. Sometimes I have wondered how diligently soul-winners would work to lead people to Jesus if every convert had to join some other congregation! Few congregations reach out to help other congregations that are faltering financially. Helping other congregations in time of need is part of the pattern for a New Testament church.

PUT SPIRITUAL GIFTS TO USE

Paul dealt in detail with the issue of spiritual gifts in 1 Cor 12–14. Some distinguish sharply between a talent and a spiritual gift. The apostle Paul never raised that issue. More, the list given is exemplary, not exhaustive. There may be other spiritual gifts not listed here or elsewhere in the New Testament. At Corinth, spiritual gifts had become a problem because the congregation abused them. Here, Paul pointed out that the Spirit gives gifts to every believer (1 Cor 12:7); that the Spirit gives different gifts to individual believers (1 Cor 12:8–11); and that the Spirit means everyone should use their gifts for the health and growth of the body, i.e., the church (1

Cor 12:12–31). Rather than misusing or ignoring gifts the Spirit gives, Paul called the Corinthians to recognize and use them as God meant them to be used.

Did they? No one knows. But if they did, it would set a pattern for the making of a New Testament church. All too few congregations emphasize utilizing spiritual gifts. Most do not help their members identify their spiritual gifts. Many have no plan to give their members a chance to use their gifting. In my earlier days as a pastor, when someone came down the aisle asking for membership in my church, I would ask them to be seated while someone got information from them. I stopped doing that. Far too many mistook my words, "Be seated on the front row," as the Great Commission. They sat down and never got up! So I started asking them to remain standing at my side as the invitation continued. And my word to them became, "We are going to find your spiritual gifts and put you to work!" Highlighting spiritual gifts so that every member gets a chance to use his gifting is part of the pattern for a New Testament church!

GIVE PROPORTIONATELY

"Now concerning the collection for the saints" (1 Cor 16:1) shows this was one of the questions the Corinthians asked in their letter to Paul. The historical situation is well-documented. Poverty was chronic in Jerusalem. This crisis was caused by a famine (Acts 11:27–30), by persecution (Acts 8:1; 1 Thess 2:14; Heb 10:34), and by their sale of assets to help care for converts from Pentecost to stay over in the city to learn the fundamentals of their new-found faith in Jesus of Nazareth (Acts 4:34–35). The people were impoverished and hurting. Paul told the Corinthians how to take an offering to meet this need. Among other things, he stressed that every member should give "as he may prosper" (1 Cor 16:2). What a Christian gives to God must be based on what God has given to him. If God gives much, he expects much in return. If he gives less, he expects less. Giving should be according to blessing!

Some people started giving God twenty dollars a week years ago. Even though they now make much more money, they still give only twenty dollars! The "as-he-may-prosper" principle demands they give much more. A good proportion is a tithe, i.e., the first 10 percent of a person's income. It is misguided to dismiss the tithe as an Old Testament thing commanded under the law. Remember that Jesus said it should be done (Matt 23:23). And it is hard to see that anyone should give less under grace than under the law. In fact, giving ought to go beyond tithing if God prospers much. As a young man, R. G. LeTourneau, founder of LeTourneau University in Longview, Texas, started tithing. But he kept on raising the proportion as God blessed his business more and more until at last he was giving God 90 percent of his income and living on the 10 percent left.[1] It is not that everyone should rush out and begin giving 90 percent. But the pattern for a New Testament church is proportional giving—giving more as God gives more. Tithing is a good way to do it.

A pattern for a New Testament church includes stressing unity, practicing church discipline, settling disputes internally, living a godly life, helping others in need, encouraging the use of spiritual gifts, and giving as God blesses!

1. Challies, "Philanthropists."

Chapter 9

The Misled Churches
Galatia

THIS IS THE ONLY letter Paul addressed to a group of churches, "the churches of Galatia" (Gal 1:2). Also, he called his readers "Galatians" (Gal 3:1). This language makes for a problem because in the first century AD, "Galatia" was used in two different ways. In its ethnic sense, Galatia referred to an area in north-central Asia Minor (near modern Ankara, Turkey), which had been occupied in the third century BC by people of Celtic background from Gaul (hence "Gaul-atia"). In its political sense, Galatia was a province Rome created in 25 BC when it consolidated the original Galatian kingdom with large areas to the south, extending almost to the Mediterranean Sea. This province contained Pisidian Antioch, Iconium, Derbe, and Lystra. To which Galatia did Paul write? Was it to churches in the smaller area originally settled by ethnic Gauls in the north? Or was it to churches in the larger area including new territory in the south? Paul visited the southern area on his first missionary trip (Acts 13:13– 14:27) and attended the Jerusalem conference on his return (Acts 15). If he ever made it to the northern area and founded churches there, it was on his second missionary trip (Acts 16:6), before he crossed the Aegean to Macedonia and Achaia.

Perhaps the answer is found in the fact that Paul customarily used provincial rather than ethnic names.[1] Maybe this tendency confirms the South Galatian theory and so gives a clue as to the exact churches involved. Acts records Paul's ministry that led to converts, and presumably local churches, in Antioch of Pisidia (Acts 13:42–48), Iconium (Acts 14:4–6), Lystra (Acts 14:8–12), and Derbe (Acts 14:20). On his second (Acts 15:41) and third (Acts 16:1–6; 18:23) missionary trips, the apostle revisited those congregations.

These churches Paul founded had been misled by false teachers and were headed down a path to doctrinal deviation. He found it necessary to write a stern letter to them, a missive in which readers find little positive content. Then what justifies including the Galatian churches, about which Paul had nothing good to say, in a treatment of patterns for building a New Testament church? Simply this: Paul's statements suggest patterns a congregation can follow to establish a New Testament church.

ACCEPT GOD'S CHOICE TO LEAD THE CHURCH

Clearly God wanted Paul in Galatia. The man wanted to preach in provincial Asia and Bithynia, but the Holy Spirit shut him up and sent him to Phrygia and Galatia (Acts 16:6–7). The Lord had need of him among the Galatians and so marked out Paul's path into those areas. Remarkably, the Galatians received Paul as if he were an angel or Jesus Christ himself (Gal 4:14). Bear in mind that Paul was not a pretty boy! He may even have been the homeliest of all the apostles. Early Christian traditions describe him as being short in stature and not particularly attractive in appearance. He himself said he was not eloquent (1 Cor 2:1) and suffered some kind of physical ailment, a "thorn in the flesh," likely an eye problem (Gal

---

1. Paul mentioned churches in the provinces of Achaia (1 Cor 16:15; 2 Cor 9:2), Asia (1 Cor 16:19; 2 Tim 1:15), and Macedonia (2 Cor 8:1). Also, he referred to the broad regions of Syria and Cilicia (Gal 1:21), Illyricum (Rom 15:19), and Dalmatia (2 Tim 4:10).

4:15). Also, Paul was single (1 Cor 7:8), which some believe makes a man unfit to serve as a pastor. But the Galatians recognized in him God's man for the hour and fell in line behind him.

Paul might have found it hard to get a call from many modern congregations who prefer a preacher who cuts a striking figure, is a polished orator, and sports a beautiful wife. Too many make too much of the prospective pastor's physical appearance, his way with words, and his wife. Does he have a lazy eye or use glasses with thick lenses? Is he fat? Is he unimpressively short? Is he ugly? Are his table manners not up to par? Is he married? It is so wrong to estimate a man's worth by how he looks and speaks, what he wears, and whether he has a wife, instead of whether he may be God's man for the job.

A congregation must be sensitive enough to the voice of God to identify the Lord's man to be their pastor, regardless of all secondary matters. That sensitivity is part of a pattern for making a New Testament church.

GUARD AGAINST FALSE TEACHERS

Satan is a liar and the father of lies. The dark lord who deceived Eve in Eden has used false teachers ever since to trick people and lead them into error. The church must always be on guard against heresy and reject those who teach it. However, these Galatian churches had let false teachers in and listened to them. And those false teachers led them astray! Paul said the Galatian believers were turning from the gospel of grace to "another" gospel that was not really a gospel at all (Gal 1:6–9). Possibly, the heretics were Judaizers who said gentiles had to become Jewish proselytes to access salvation through the Jewish Messiah, Jesus, or had to keep the law in order to "be made perfect" (Gal 3:3–5), i.e., mature as Christians. Almost unbelievably, these false teachers had "quickly" (Gal 1:6) perverted the gospel of grace as Paul preached it. And the heresy had impacted several churches in the area. Of a false teacher Paul said, "Let him be accursed" (Gal 1:9).

A New Testament church must always be on guard against heresy. Some false teachers are people no one would suspect were teaching theological error. These teachers and preachers serve in and/or were trained by denominational (in this case, Southern Baptist) schools. I can recall one professor at a Baptist college offered to a student this explanation of the Trinity: "I am a son, a husband, and a father. There is one God who fills the roles of Father, Son and Spirit." His view was condemned as heretical centuries ago. Though I will withhold names and titles, I can also recall the president of a Baptist university who published a book in which he denied that Jesus is God, insisted that Jesus is not to be worshiped, rejected the idea that Jesus is the only Savior, and scoffed at the notion that faith in Jesus is essential for salvation. A professor at a Baptist seminary argued ardently with me that, if believing in the virgin birth is not essential to salvation (a statement with which I agreed, because a six-year-old who has no idea what a virgin is can give his heart to Jesus), then believing in the virgin birth of Jesus is not important at all. (Wrong! It is important to believe all that Scripture affirms about Jesus!) In a class I attended in seminary, my professor denied that Jesus died as a substitute for our sins. In his judgment, if God gave up his son to the cross, it was child abuse. A professor at another Baptist seminary frankly stated that he did not believe Jesus rose from the dead bodily. All these men taught in, or were trained in, Southern Baptist institutions. Many Southern Baptists would have trusted them to speak truth and followed them blindly. Sad to say, that same situation obtains across denominational lines!

Often, false teachers waver on the absolute essentials of the gospel, i.e., that salvation comes by grace alone, through faith alone, in Jesus Christ alone. And often they recognize a source of authority alongside or even above the Bible, e.g., the Book of Mormon, the visions of Henry C. Kinley, the writings of the Watchtower Bible and Tract Society, or the booklets produced by the Unity School of Christianity.

In his essay "Warnings to the Churches," J. C. Ryle, a nineteenth-century bishop in the Church of England, wrote about how bad it is for a church to be roiled by controversy. "But," he added, "there is one thing which is even worse than controversy, and that is *false doctrine tolerated, allowed, and permitted* without protest."[2] He also said that "there are three things which men never ought to trifle with: a little poison, a little false doctrine, and a little sin."[3]

To be a New Testament church, a congregation must maintain constant vigilance against false teachers and tolerate no false doctrine!

MATCH GRACE WITH WORKS

Most scholars agree that Paul aimed the letter to the Galatians against a message that mixed works with grace. In it, he forcefully maintained that both salvation (Gal 2:15–16) and sanctification (Gal 3:2–3) come by grace through faith alone, not by any works. This was to correct the views of the false teachers already mentioned. In fact, if the Galatians depended on circumcision, either as a means of gaining acceptance with God or of growing to Christian maturity, they had "fallen away from grace" (Gal 5:4), i.e., fallen back toward works, making grace null and void. However, as Paul continued, the grace of God that saves and sanctifies leads God's people to good works (Gal 6:4, 9–10). It is not a matter of "either/or" but of "both/and"—grace and works!

It is quite unbiblical to drown out the call to good works by crying "faith alone" so loudly. The New Testament calls for both. Even Paul, a hard-nosed advocate for faith alone, recognized this. In other places, he wrote that salvation comes by grace through faith but that Christians are "created in Christ Jesus for good works, which God prepared beforehand, that we should walk in them" (Eph 2:8–10). He also wrote that "the grace of God has appeared" and the Savior gave himself "to redeem us from all lawlessness and to purify for himself a people for his own possession who are zealous for good works" (Titus 2:13–14).

2. Ryle, "Warnings."
3. Ryle, "Warnings."

To be a New Testament church a congregation must give equal stress to grace and the works that flow from the work of grace in a man's life! A New Testament church follows the pattern of finding God's leader for the job, fighting false teachers, and working out the faith within.

Chapter 10

The Mission Church
Samaria

THE STONING OF STEPHEN set off a wave of persecution against Christians in Jerusalem. For some undisclosed reason, the apostles stayed in the city, but other believers scattered throughout Judea and Samaria. Wherever these Christians went, they gossiped the gospel (Acts 8:1–4; 11:19).

One of the first seven deacons (Acts 6:5), Philip by name, made his way to the city of Samaria, capital of the ancient kingdom of Samaria. Herod the Great had renamed it Sebaste, which is Greek for "Augustus," the emperor he wished to honor by that act. The city stood on a hilltop about seven miles northwest of Shechem. There was bad blood between Samaritans and Jews. Jews considered Samaritans racial and religious half-breeds; Samaritans hated Jews in return. Jews considered the region of Samaria a polluted place. When they found it necessary to go from Galilee to Judea, many Jewish travelers crossed the Jordan and went down a much longer eastern route to avoid Samaria altogether. These prejudices were deeply ingrained, but the gospel broke through them. A Jew came to share the gospel with the Samaritans, and numerous Samaritans "received the word of God" (Acts 8:14) when Philip declared it.

It is reasonable to assume that Philip led these converts to form a church. If he did, it would make the church at Samaria the first church on record planted by Jerusalem Christians, i.e., the first mission church (Acts 8:1–25). From Luke's description of that ministry and that mission, some patterns for a New Testament church emerge.

CHANGED PEOPLE'S LIVES

Miracles marked Philip's ministry in the city (Acts 8:6–7). By the power of God, he cast out unclean spirits from those oppressed by demons. He made cripples whole and caused the lame to leap. The change in those delivered and healed by the power of God was obvious for all the people to see.

This present age may not be an era known for miracles such as exorcisms and public healings. But a New Testament church must still be known for a ministry that miraculously changes lives. Through the power of the Holy Spirit here and now, a life can be redirected, a home rearranged, an addiction ended, or the chains of sin broken. If lives are not changed through its Spirit-empowered ministry, such a congregation has "the appearance of godliness" but not its power (2 Tim 3:5).

Most religious activity is just the work of the world moved over into the church. It is nothing more than the power used all week in the workaday world, but on Sunday totes a Bible and talks about God. To be a New Testament church, a congregation must be marked by how its gospel ministry changes lives!

PRACTICED BELIEVER'S IMMERSION

At Samaria, a person who became a believer was "baptized" (Acts 8:12). Baptism was the first act in what was meant to be a lifetime of obedience to the Lord Jesus who had commanded it (Matt 28:19).

The verb is a form of *baptizo*, from which comes the English word "baptize." The root *bapt-* means "to dip in or under, to submerge, to immerse." So the word itself calls for submersion in water. How strange that some congregations now sprinkle or pour water on new Christians instead of immersing them! There are other good Greek words for sprinkle (*rantizo*) and for pour (*epicheo*). Therefore, to sprinkle is to "rantize" but not to baptize. And to pour is to "epichize" but not to baptize. If the Lord ordered immersion, as he did, nothing else is acceptable for a New Testament church.

Despite my high regard for my fellow-Baptist Wayne Grudem, he stepped way out of line in his suggestion that, in the interest of Christian unity, it may be time to lay aside insistence on believer's immersion and accept and teach sprinkling and pouring, even that of infants![1] My response? No one has a right to change the New Testament way of obeying the Lord's commands. Would God have accepted oak instead of the gopher wood (cypress) he ordered Noah to use to build the ark (Gen 6:14)? Partial obedience is full disobedience! Full obedience demands immersing believers. To be a New Testament church, a congregation must practice the New Testament practice of immersion.

PRIORITIZED LAY MINISTRY

The leaders in the Samaritan church-plant were not folks who made ministry their profession but people who earned their living in some secular job while they "gossiped the gospel." All the apostles stayed in Jerusalem. Philip was a deacon. He and other common people just made it their business to do the work of the ministry in Samaria. That is how it worked for this New Testament church.

From somewhere people got the idea that a church hires a pastor or staff to do the work of the ministry. That notion did not come from the New Testament. Instead, the New Testament says God gifted the church with pastors and teachers in order "to equip the saints for the work of the ministry" (Eph 4:12). The pastor and staff are responsible to feed and lead laymen and

1. Grudem, *Systematic*, 982–83.

women and train them to do the work of the ministry! It is the congregation's job to minister!

For more than twenty years during my tenure at the University of Mobile, I recruited, trained, and led groups of students and local church members to help various mission congregations in Brazil. How refreshing it was on one visit to Lagoa Santa, a suburb of Belo Horizonte, to find a fellowship led by two Brazilian pilots stationed at a nearby air force base! Trained by their respective former pastors, these two laymen were giving direction and training to this pastorless congregation. The people were growing as believers and reaching their community with the gospel! Laymen led the way!

The point is not that having a pastor keeps a congregation from becoming a New Testament church. It is rather that, in a New Testament church, the members take responsibility for the work of the ministry rather than trying to hire staff to do that work for them!

MARKED BY GREAT JOY

"So there was much joy in that city," reported Luke (Acts 8:8). This was the impact of the gospel on the lives of believers! Early Christians rejoiced "with joy inexpressible" (1 Pet 1:8), that is, a strange joy that cannot be put into words or cannot be exhausted by words. There is a popular story about an alleged letter often attributed to Cyprian, bishop of Carthage in the third century AD, written to his young friend Donatus. He may not have actually penned this paragraph but it reflects reality, and according to the story it went something like this:

> This is a bad world, Donatus, an incredibly bad world. But I have discovered in the midst of it a quiet and holy people who have learned a great secret. They have found a joy, which is a thousand times better than any pleasure of arts and full life. They are despised and persecuted, but they do not care. They are masters of their souls. They

have overcome the world. These people, Donatus, are the Christians and I am one of them.

Samaritan believers were filled with incredible joy like that!

It has been left to modern believers to make the Christian life dull, dry, and dreary! Well might one ask of multitudes of congregations, "Where is the joy you knew when first you saw the Lord?" Little joy is evident; just a glimmer now and then. For many, living for Jesus is more a chore or a duty and often boring. Is there any joy in your life? Is there any joy in your church?

To be a New Testament church a congregation should exhibit the power of God to change lives, immerse believers, make much of lay leadership, and rejoice with the joy of the Lord!

Conclusion

A NEWLY-HIRED SALESMAN'S FIRST sales report to the home office stunned management. Clearly Gooch lacked language skills. This is what he wrote:

> I seen this outfit in New Yorke which they ain't never bought a dimes wurth of nothing from us, and I sole them couple hundred thousand dollars of guds. Now I am going to Chcawgo.

Before the sales manager could give Gooch the heave-ho, along came another report from Chicago:

> I cum hyar and sole them half a millyon.

Fearful if he did not fire the illiterate peddler, and fearful if he did, the sales manager dumped the problem in the lap of the company president. The following morning, all employees were flabbergasted to see both reports posted on the bulletin board outside the CEO's office with this note from the boss tacked above:

> We bin spending far two much time trying to spel instead of trying to sel. Lets watch those sails. I want everybody should read these reports from Gooch who is on the rode doing a grate job for us. Now lets all go out and due like he done![1]

1. This is my adaptation of a story told in Maxwell, *Developing the Leader*, 8–9.

What I've described in the previous chapters are some patterns from New Testament churches. "Now lets all go out and due like they done!"

Bibliography

Challies, Tim. "The Philanthropists: R. G. LeTourneau." Oct. 20, 2013. https://www.challies.com/philanthropists/the-philanthropists-r-g-letourneau/.

George, Timothy. "Dr. Luther's Theology." *Christian History* 34 (1992) 18–21.

Grey, J. D. "The Pastor—Undershepherd of the Flock." *Louisiana Baptist Message*. June 13, 1974.

Grudem, Wayne. *Systematic Theology*. Grand Rapids: Zondervan, 1994.

International Churchill Society. "Russia." June 24, 2023. https://winstonchurchill.org/resources/quotes/the-worst-form-of-government/.

———. "The Worst Form of Government." Feb. 25, 2016. https://winstonchurchill.org/resources/quotes/the-worst-form-of-government/.

Juvenal. "Satire 3." Translated by G. G. Ramsay. https://www.tertullian.org/fathers/juvenal_satires_03.htm.

Maxwell, John C. *Developing the Leader Within You*. Nashville: Thomas Nelson, 1993.

McDaniel, George W. *The Churches of the New Testament*. Nashville: Sunday School Board of the Southern Baptist Convention, 1921.

Nieuwhof, Carey. "Church Giving Statistics for 2025: Who's Giving, When, and How Much?" https://careynieuwhof.com/church-giving-statistics/.

Pierce, Earle V. *The Supreme Beatitude*. New York: Revell, 1948.

Powell, Paul. *The Church Today*. Dallas: Annuity Board of the Southern Baptist Convention, 1997.

Rogers, Cleon L., Jr., and Cleon L. Rogers III. *The New Linguistic and Exegetical Key to the Greek Testament*. Grand Rapids: Zondervan, 1998.

Ryle, J. C. "Warnings to the Churches." Monergism, July 2015. https://www.monergism.com/thethreshold/sdg/ryle/Warnings%20to%20the%20Churches%20-%20J.%20C.%20Ryle.pdf.

Williams, Charles. *The New Testament in the Language of the People*. Chicago: Moody, 1972.

.

www.ingramcontent.com/pod-product-compliance
Lightning Source LLC
Chambersburg PA
CBHW070023110426
42741CB00034B/2443